The Dharmic Path to Innovation

OrangeBooks Publication

1st Floor, Rajhans Arcade, Mall Road, Kohka, Bhilai, Chhattisgarh 490020
Website: **www.orangebooks.in**

First Edition, 2025

ISBN: 978-93-6554-496-1

Price: Rs. 272.00

Printed in India

The Dharmic Path to Innovation

108 Timeless Lessons from Hindu Thought for Disrupting the Modern World

Sachin Rustagi

OrangeBooks Publication
www.orangebooks.in

Dedication

To my beloved children, Tulsi and Surya,

May this book become a seed in your **hearts**—a guide not just for how to create, but how to create with purpose.

In a world where Artificial Intelligence (AI) will shape much of what you see, touch, and do, I hope you'll remember this:

It's not just about what you build, but why you build it.

Let this be your compass for a life of courage, clarity, and dharma— so you grow into innovators who don't just chase the future, but help shape it with integrity.

Because in this coming age you will either augment your human-centered wisdom with AI, or be driven by it without choice.

Choose to drive. Choose to lead.

Choose to create from your dharmic core. Dharmo Rakshati Rakshitah (Manusmriti verse 8.15).

With all my love,

Dad-oo

Introduction

Reclaiming the Dharmic Core of Innovation

Let's be real for a second.

In this fast-moving AI-driven world where we obsess over algorithms, dashboards, and unicorn valuations, it's easy to forget one thing: innovation has always been human first and relative to the past. Before the KPIs, before the whiteboards, before the AI—there was someone, somewhere, who paused, got curious, and took a risk. No guarantees. No roadmap. Just a gut feeling and a little spark.

That's where this book begins.

This isn't another how-to guide stuffed with frameworks and acronyms. It's a reminder—a reset. Innovation isn't just some corporate strategy or buzzword on a slide deck It's a rhythm. A way of being. It starts with curiosity, gets messy with experimentation, and if we're lucky, ends in a moment of clarity and growth.

And here's the cool part: this rhythm isn't new. Long before "innovation labs" and "design sprints," cultures—especially ancient ones like the Dharmic and Hindu civilization; already knew how to do this. They played, they POC'd (aka prototyped), they learned. Whether it was a Guru or Rishi (aka sage) meditating in a forest or a village woman turning waste into utility, the spirit of experimentation was everywhere. It wasn't flashy. But it was real. And sacred.

Now, look, I get it—we live in an age of AI and automation. The world's changing faster than ever. But amidst all the tech and tools, something's getting lost. We're forgetting the heart. The wonder. The reflection. We build these amazing systems, but sometimes we forget to ask: *What's the soul behind this solution?*

That's why this book exists. To help us bring the human back into how we create, lead, and grow. To help us reclaim that space where ideas are allowed to stumble, questions are allowed to linger, and people—real, messy, brilliant people—are allowed to show up fully.

So if you're looking for permission to slow down, question more, and tap into that ancient, creative part of yourself—you've found the right place.

This journey is personal. It's cultural. It's spiritual. But it's also wildly practical. Each chapter offers stories and practices you can try—whether you're leading a team, launching a product, or just figuring out what's next in life.

You don't need to follow everything perfectly. This isn't a checklist. It's more like a foundation. Let it guide you back to the part of innovation that's deeply human and from within -- unshakably wise, and still very much alive.

Welcome to the rhythm of Dharmic Innovation. Let's make it meaningful.

Contents

Chapter - 1

Daily Innovation

Everyday Dharma for Everyday Innovation

Leveraging What We've Always Known

Innovation isn't always born in labs or born from code—it often starts in the dusty corners of tradition, where old wisdom meets everyday creativity. In a world shaped by AI, automation, and rapid change, the need for human-centered, intuitive innovation is greater than ever. And sometimes, the answers lie not in Silicon Valley Tel Aviv, New York or Toronto, but in a craft fair in Uttar Pradesh, a temple ritual in Tamil Nadu, or a story passed down through the Ramayana.

This chapter is an exploration of how Hindu culture, rich philosophy, and everyday practices can become fuel for the future. We're going to look at how rangoli designs, folk art, sacred rituals, and the avatars of Vishnu can teach us to design better products, spark more imaginative thinking, and build organizations that adapt with grace. Each section unpacks a principle, not as a lecture, but as a conversation—a walk through our shared cultural memory that ends in a modern insight. These stories are designed to be both personal and practical—rooted in dharma, yet aimed at innovation.

So whether you're a product manager, founder, designer, or just someone stuck on a creative plateau—let's go on this ride together. Keep your mind open, your curiosity sharp, and your respect for the ancient alive. Because innovation isn't always about what's next. Sometimes, it's about remembering what we've always known.

1. Practice Daily Unstructured Creativity

Imagine waking up in a quiet South Indian village. The sun is just stretching over the palm trees, and on every threshold, women and men, both young and old, are on the floor, hand-drawing intricate kolams—sacred geometric patterns made with rice flour. These designs are not judged, not critiqued, not even preserved. They are drawn anew every morning and washed away by evening. This daily ritual is a celebration of impermanence, intuition, and mindfulness—without pressure, perfection, or performance.

Now think of our workplaces. Most of our creativity is task-driven, goal-bound, and hyper-scheduled. What if we borrowed the kolam mindset? Each morning at work—or even just at your desk—take five minutes to sketch, doodle, or write a few wild ambitious ideas. It doesn't need to be good. It doesn't need to be anything. Just flow. Just like kolams aren't drawn to be framed, your sketches don't need to win awards. But they *will* unlock neural highways that lead to bigger, better breakthroughs.

In fact, studies show that cognitive flexibility—our ability to switch perspectives—is strengthened through low-pressure, unstructured creative time. The brain relaxes. The subconscious steps in. Innovation becomes less forced and more fluid.

When I started encouraging my team at a mature financial services corporation to try this, it felt silly at first. But after just two weeks, our ideation sessions had a new rhythm. People were connecting dots faster, laughing more, and prototyping things they would've never voiced before.

Modern Practice Tip:

Start your mornings with five minutes of unstructured creativity—sketch, write, mind-map. Make it a ritual, not a task.

2. Study Indian Folk Art Patterns

Some of the most powerful design thinking doesn't come from design schools—it comes from dusty village walls, festival banners, and palm-leaf paintings. Folk art forms like Madhubani (Bihar), Warli (Maharashtra), and Pattachitra (Odisha) weren't just ornamental. They were storytelling mediums, ecological wisdom keepers, and social blueprints. They used geometry, repetition, and symbolism to encode generational knowledge.

Imagine a designer today studying Warli art, where circles and triangles express everything from farming to rituals. Or a brand strategist finding inspiration in Madhubani's layered storytelling to create ad campaigns that feel rooted. There's genius in these patterns—both in form and function. Each design teaches balance, flow, and cultural relevance.

At a cultural research lab in Ahmedabad, a team of young urban designers once spent three weeks living in a tribal village in Maharashtra. They weren't there to extract visuals—they were there to observe how the community used Warli motifs to communicate harvest cycles, gender roles, and even dispute resolutions. One night, during a festival, they noticed a large mural being painted—not by an artist, but by three generations of women together. The matriarch drew the sacred mountain, her daughter painted daily rituals, and the granddaughter added animals with playful twists. That image became the inspiration for an award-winning financial education app—its interface used circular progression models and pictorial prompts to explain compound interest to rural women. A pattern once drawn in rice paste became the foundation of a modern tech solution.

In a world drowning in generic design, digging into folk art can be a goldmine of differentiation. And it's not about copying—it's about decoding the thinking behind it.

Modern Practice Tip:

Deep-dive into a folk art form. Extract its patterns, logic, and symbols. Use it to inspire your design language or story frameworks.

3. Use Visual Storytelling in Business

Imagine an artist in West Bengal and Odisha holding a long-painted scroll. As they sing verses from the Ramayana in Sanskrit, they slowly unroll the scroll, revealing scenes one by one. It's called patachitra—and it's possibly India's earliest form of multimedia storytelling.

Now fast-forward to today's boardrooms, where we're often trying to explain complex tech solutions or pitch disruptive ideas. What if we told those stories visually?

What if we turned the abstract into the relatable—just like the pata artists did?

There was a design-thinking bootcamp in Bangalore where one team had to pitch an AI-powered solution for rural healthcare delivery. Instead of a standard slide deck, they used a visual diary: a large paper mural that unfolded as they narrated the journey of a fictional village elder named Savitri. Scene by scene, the mural showed her challenges—delayed diagnoses, long travel, unfamiliar urban hospitals—and how the proposed app connected local clinics to AI-backed diagnostics. The audience, a mix of investors and healthcare professionals, didn't just understand the idea—they felt it. The team didn't just raise funds; they also got unexpected offers for pilot programs in two states. Their visuals didn't simplify the tech—they humanized it.

This is not about being childish. It's about being clear. When visuals and narratives dance together, people feel engaged, not talked at. In the world of AI and data, visual storytelling is a humanizing superpower.

Modern Practice Tip:

Next time you pitch, try using a visual narrative. Comics, journey maps, or storyboards beat bullet points any day.

4. Zero Budget Innovation Challenges

Remember the Mahabharata scene where Arjuna's chariot wheel breaks? Krishna doesn't panic. He lifts a broken wheel, turns it into a weapon, and marches on. That's jugaad—the desi spirit of "make do or make new." It's frugal, fast, and fearless.

In a university in Chennai, a group of engineering students once entered a national innovation contest with no budget, no lab access, and just one broken laptop between them. Their challenge? Build a prototype for flood-warning tech. They scavenged wires from old cassette players, waterproofed sensors using plastic bottles and candle wax, and tested everything in a borrowed fish tank. Their pitch video was shot on a borrowed phone and edited overnight in a cyber café. And yet, their solution outperformed teams backed by grants and mentorships. Why? Because they designed for real-life constraints, not textbook perfection. That spirit—working with what's at hand and never waiting for ideal conditions—is pure *jugaad* .It reminded me of how Indian street vendors rig biscuit tins into speaker systems, or how rural kids turn old tires into toys. Constraint breeds creativity. When resources are tight, imagination steps up.

So many AI startups are bootstrapping today. They don't need VC funding to innovate—they need Krishna-style cleverness.

Modern Practice Tip:

Run a zero-budget challenge in your team. Restrict materials and time. Watch creativity explode.

5. Divergent Thinking with Common Objects

What can you do with a coconut shell? In Indian homes, it's a bowl. A ladle. A bird feeder. A toy. Even a musical instrument. That's not just reuse—it's imaginative repurposing.

Divergent thinking is the ability to see multiple possibilities for a single stimulus. In AI product design, it's gold. The more ways you can view an object or concept, the more likely you are to find disruptive paths.

There was a rural innovation fair in Karnataka where local schoolchildren were given just one object: an old bicycle wheel. No prompts, no instructions. Over two hours, they turned it into a pulley system to lift water buckets, a spinning scoreboard for a cricket game, a rotating classroom timetable, and even a ceiling fan using hand-cranked power. The judges—engineers from an urban incubator—were stunned. None of the children had ever been taught "design thinking," yet their instinctive creativity, honed by growing up with limited toys and tools, far outpaced their urban counterparts. It was divergent thinking in its purest, most joyful form.

Everyday Indian life—especially in rural areas—is a masterclass in divergent thinking. It teaches that one form can wear many functions, if you just shift your view.

Modern Practice Tip:

Take a random object. List 10 possible uses in 5 minutes. Do this weekly with your team to strengthen idea elasticity.

6. Draw From Craft Fairs Or Haats

Let me take you on a walk through Dilli Haat or maybe a temple-side mela in Odisha during the popular Ratha

Yatra. The air is thick with the scent of incense, sizzling snacks, and a thousand conversations. But hidden in these bustling crowds are stalls run by craftspeople who are quietly solving modern problems with ancient techniques. You'll see bamboo baskets reimagined as laptop carriers, terracotta pots being sold with ergonomic handles, and natural dye clothes with QR codes stitched into their tags. This isn't just tradition. It's innovation breathing in rhythm with culture.

What's wild is that most of these artisans have never studied product design or attended innovation bootcamps. Yet, they adapt year after year—based on what the customer needs, what the environment allows, and what the community values. That is *living design thinking.* And what's more, they don't waste. They reuse, upcycle, and create circular economy models out of sheer instinct.

At the Surajkund Mela in Haryana, a leather artisan from Rajasthan had re-engineered a traditional *jutti* (footwear) design for bikers. He noticed city customers hesitating to buy because the sole wore out fast on concrete. So, he began lining the bottom with scrap tire rubber from puncture shops—adding grip, durability, and a striking aesthetic. A product manager from a European footwear brand happened to be browsing and spent an hour sketching the construction. Two years later, the brand launched a "desert rider" collection inspired by this exact mix of tradition and utility. That artisan didn't just make shoes—he prototyped a global trend from a stall without Wi-Fi.

So, here's a practice I swear by: visit a fair, not for shopping, but for sourcing *ideas*. Observe how people display, bundle, explain. Ask questions. Sketch things. You'll walk away with insights you didn't know you needed.

Modern Practice Tip:

Schedule regular visits to traditional markets or fairs. Use them as real-world case studies for frugal design, sustainability, and storytelling.

7. Myth-Metaphor Design Challenges

What if Indra had an app in 2025? Would it forecast emotions instead of weather? Or consider Arjuna's bow—how might it look if built with smart tech and AI sensors? These aren't just fun questions. They're gateways to unlocking imaginative, metaphor-rich innovation.

Indian mythology isn't just narrative—it's a design brief wrapped in poetry. Gods, weapons, vehicles, even garments all serve symbolic and functional purposes. When we reframe those stories through modern lenses, we're not being whimsical—we're accessing the same creative energy that designed them in the first place.

At a design residency in Pune, participants were once given an unusual brief: choose any object from Hindu mythology and reimagine it for today's most pressing problems. One group chose *Kumbha*—the mythic pot used to store *amrita*, the nectar of immortality. Their version? A smart water container for drought-prone areas that filters, stores, and dispenses water in precise microdoses based on humidity and temperature. It used

passive cooling materials inspired by traditional *matkas* and integrated a low-cost solar chip for rural areas. What started as a myth metaphor became a serious sustainability pitch—one that later got prototyped in a government innovation challenge for water conservation.

Metaphors are powerful because they tap into emotion, memory, and archetypes. They make abstract ideas sticky. Think about how Apple used the 'desktop' metaphor for the GUI—it wasn't literal, but it was intuitive. Hindu myths are full of such metaphors waiting to be reimagined.

Modern Practice Tip:

Pick a mythic character or object. Ask your team to reimagine it as a modern product or system. It opens up symbolic, futuristic, and emotionally resonant innovation.

8. Workspace Decoration Rituals

In southern India, during Ayudha Puja, people decorate and bless their tools—ploughs, pens, even computers. It's a celebration of gratitude toward the instruments that help us thrive. Now imagine treating your laptop, your whiteboard, your code editor with that same energy. What if every quarter, your team took time to honor the tools that make their brilliance possible?

This isn't superstition. It's neuropsychology. Personalizing a workspace, decorating it with intention, and creating rituals of respect elevates the way we use our tools. It cultivates responsibility and pride. It makes work *matter* more.

At a co-working space in Coimbatore, a small fintech startup began a unique practice inspired by Ayudha Puja. Every three months, instead of a quarterly review meeting, they hosted a “Tool Day.” Desks were cleared and decorated with flowers, hand-written thank-you notes to team tools were exchanged, and even the office router got adorned with turmeric and vermilion. But more than the rituals, something deeper emerged — people began naming the exact tools that helped them solve problems: “This whiteboard helped crack our pricing model,” or “This shared doc held our first investor pitch.” One intern wrote a poem for the terminal window she used to deploy code. A visiting angel investor, witnessing the ritual, later remarked that it was the first time he saw a team that “knew how to love their process, not just their product.”

In a world of remote work and digital fatigue, rituals can rehumanize the workspace. Think less corporate clutter, more intentional energy. Think of it like putting prana back into your tools.

Modern Practice Tip:

Encourage teams to personalize and decorate their workspace every few months. Pair it with a reflection ritual—what tools helped you grow? What will you honor this quarter?

9. Multi-Sensory Ideation Rooms

Ever walked into a temple and noticed how every sense comes alive? The ringing bell, the cool stone under your feet, the smell of camphor, the sight of flickering lamps, the chants echoing in rhythm—it's a full-body reset. That's not just spiritual—it's sensory genius. And it's exactly what our ideation rooms lack.

Most brainstorming happens under white fluorescent lights, in dry air, with squeaky markers. That's cognitive constipation. We need spaces that activate our intuitive side—spaces that let the subconscious play.

At a design studio in Auroville (USA), a visiting team of software engineers once ran a week-long product sprint. But instead of booking meeting rooms, they were guided to a mud-walled meditation hall repurposed for the workshop. The space had soft floor seating, windows that opened to birdsong, subtle sandalwood scent in the corners, and warm lamps instead of overhead lights. Mornings began with silent reflection, and mid-day breaks featured walk-and-talks in the gardens. On day three, one coder broke down in tears—not from stress, but from sudden emotional clarity about a long-stuck UX problem. The team called it their most "emotionally honest" ideation sprint. What had changed wasn't the content—it was the container. The senses had been invited into the creative process.

The difference was night and day. People stayed longer. They were more present. One team even said the room felt like a "creative ashram."

The brain processes sensory inputs faster than language. So, if you want faster, richer, deeper ideas—build spaces that awaken all the senses.

Modern Practice Tip:

Rethink your innovation spaces. Use lighting, textures, sounds, and scents to create immersive zones that spark right-brain thinking.

10. Challenge Norms With Mythic Thinking

Vishnu didn't stay the same form during his appearances on Earth. He became Matsya in a flood, Rama in a kingdom, Krishna in a battlefield, and Kalki in the future. Each avatar wasn't just a form—it was a response. A bold, context-aware innovation. That's dharmic agility.

In a fast-changing world—especially in AI—we need that same energy. If your product, brand, or identity isn't evolving, it's dissolving. The question isn't "how do we stay the same?" It's "how do we become what the world needs next?"

At a social impact accelerator in Hyderabad, one youth-led climate initiative found itself losing steam. Their messaging—focused on technical jargon about carbon credits—wasn't resonating with the public. During a myth-inspired workshop, a mentor posed a question: "If your mission were an avatar of Vishnu, which would it be—and why?" One participant said, "We've been talking like Parashurama—angry and exacting. Maybe it's time we channel Krishna—strategic, playful, persuasive." That sparked a shift. Their next campaign used street theatre, humor, and gamified challenges to raise awareness about air pollution. Engagement soared. School kids participated. A municipal officer called it "the first fun climate campaign" he'd seen. They didn't change their mission—they changed their form to suit the yuga they were in.

Mythic thinking isn't about fantasy. It's about archetypes, time cycles, and transformation. It helps teams zoom out from quarterly goals to timeless relevance.

Modern Practice Tip:

During major pivots, run a "Vishnu Avatar" session. Ask: What would our product become in a different age, place, or mindset? Let dharma guide the reinvention.

Conclusion

Across these principles, we've seen how a dharmic worldview can open up refreshing possibilities for innovation. From the bustling lanes of craft fairs to the silent awe of temple spaces, from the metaphorical genius of myths to the reverent decorating of workspaces—each practice gives us a new lens to see, feel, and build. These aren't just cultural artifacts. They're design frameworks, strategic prompts, and human-centered ideation tools disguised in ritual and story.

The modern world tends to separate the spiritual from the strategic, the mythical from the practical. But Hindu tradition never did that. Vishnu changed forms to stay relevant. Artisans reinvented tools year after year. Senses were honored to sharpen the mind. That's not ancient thinking—it's timeless innovation.

The challenge now is yours. How can you ritualize reverence in your workspaces? How can your product evolve like an avatar in a new yuga? How can you design spaces that speak to your senses, not just your KPIs? You don't need a bigger budget—you need a deeper imagination. And for that, look no further than your own roots.

Practice Recap:

- Visit traditional markets for hands-on, frugal design lessons.
- Reimagine mythological tools as modern products.
- Personalize and bless your workspace each quarter.
- Build sensory-rich innovation environments.
- Use avatar thinking to pivot and rebrand with purpose.

This isn't about going backward—it's about going inward to go forward. Let dharma guide your disruption.

Chapter - 2

Harmonized Collaboration

Harnessing Ancient Harmony for Future Innovation

Introduction: Why Collaboration Is Sacred Ground

Innovation is not a solo act. It never has been.

Whether you're in a boardroom in downtown Toronto or on a rooftop in Bengaluru coding until sunrise, the greatest breakthroughs don't happen in isolation. They happen in *circles*—in spaces where people feel safe enough to dream out loud, challenge each other, and build on the sparks of others. And if you look closely, Hindu traditions knew this all along.

From the open-air satsangs of the Upanishads to the rotating councils of village panchayats, collaboration wasn't just functional—it was sacred. It was dharma in action. People gathered not just to debate or decide, but to *co-create reality*. Innovation was never hoarded. It was *invited*. It was sung, danced, offered, and debated under banyan trees with cups of buttermilk and the occasional thunderclap in the distance.

In today's world—driven by speed, data, and AI—collaboration is our differentiator. It's what separates the truly adaptive organizations from the ones that just automate faster. This chapter is about tapping into the ancient wisdom of Hindu collaborative models and reframing them for your modern workspace, whether you're building the next unicorn or leading a small, passionate team trying to make something better.

So, let's go beyond brainstorming. Let's talk about building trust, rhythm, rituals, metaphors, and shared identity. Because when you innovate *together*, something bigger than all of you shows up in the room.

1. Circle-Based Dialogue Instead of Hierarchy

Let me paint a scene for you.

Imagine an ancient grove on the banks of the Ganga. Under a large banyan tree, sages gather with a few princes, merchants, and wandering seekers. There's no podium. No head of the table. Just a circle. Everyone faces each other. King Janaka, one of the wisest monarchs, sits not on a throne, but on a straw mat like everyone else. And there's Gargi—the woman sage—raising profound questions that even the learned men bow to.

This was the satsang format. A circle of inquiry. No one dominates. Everyone contributes.

Now, think about your typical Monday morning meeting. There's a head of the table. The boss speaks first. Everyone else scans for signals—what's safe to say, what's not. Ideas shrink before they're even spoken.

That's where innovation dies—when hierarchy overshadows curiosity.

At an education startup in Bengaluru, the leadership team decided to try a monthly "circle council" inspired by ancient *gurukul* discussions. No agenda, no hierarchy—just one guiding question written on a whiteboard. During one session, a 21-year-old junior intern hesitantly shared a concern about how their mobile app wasn't accessible to left-handed students. It sparked a design rethink that eventually improved usability for all users. In another, the office janitor was invited to share feedback—and pointed out a broken entry buzzer that was frustrating parents during pickups. No dashboard ever caught that.

The founders later said those circles gave them more real insight than three months of analytics reports. The room wasn't just arranged differently—it *thought* differently.

Circles aren't just shapes. They're philosophies. They say—we're equal, we're in this together, your voice matters.

Modern Practice Tip:

Next time you need bold thinking, ditch the boardroom setup. Try a circle. Try listening more than speaking. And maybe… just maybe, leave the title outside.

2. Invite Unlikely Collaborators

Ever notice how Krishna's brilliance wasn't just his strategies, but *who* he brought into the story?

He didn't just hang with the elite. He partnered with Sudama, a poor Brahmin childhood friend, showing loyalty matters more than wealth. He aligned with Hanuman, a vanara from a different realm—bridging species and worlds. Heck, even in Mahabharata, he used wisdom from Yakshas and dealt with Rakshasas when needed.

Krishna knew that true power lies in assembling a team that *no one saw coming*.

In the AI world today, we're often stuck collaborating within our comfort zones—data folks talk to data folks, designers to designers. But innovation? That's born when a poet joins a coding sprint. When a biologist sits with a blockchain dev. When someone from customer care becomes the product brainstorm lead.

At a public health hackathon in Kerala, a medical researcher teamed up with a theatre director, a sanitation worker, and a GIS mapping intern. Initially, judges were skeptical—what could this eclectic group possibly build? But by the end of 48 hours, they had created a culturally sensitive audio-visual toolkit for menstrual education, tailored for tribal communities. The theatre artist scripted the stories, the sanitation worker offered real-world insights, and the intern mapped accessibility zones. That solution won—not just for tech, but for empathy, reach, and realism. No one on a conventional dev team could've cracked it alone.

Modern Practice Tip:

Build innovation squads with the "Krishna model"—cross-realm, cross-domain, cross-level. Invite the janitor. Invite the intern. Invite the wild card.

3. Practice Shared Ritual Before Meetings

Let's shift the lens for a moment.

Imagine a design consultancy in Pune known for tight deadlines and high-pressure sprints. A few years ago, after a string of creative blocks and interpersonal tensions, the team decided to experiment with something different. Before every major meeting or ideation session, they began a ritual: two minutes of silence followed by a simple round where each person answered one question—"What's one thing you're bringing into this room today?"

Answers ranged from "excitement" to "fatigue" to "curiosity." Within weeks, something subtle changed. People listened more closely. Team leads began noticing fewer interruptions and more thoughtful contributions. One senior developer, previously withdrawn, began contributing ideas that later shaped the firm's flagship project.

Why does this matter?

Because rituals, like the *diya* before a *puja* or a *shanti mantra* before discourse, aren't fluff. They're alignment tools. They signal: we're stepping into sacred work. They bring shared presence.

In Hindu tradition, before any deep act—teaching, dialogue, even war (like Arjuna's)—there is preparation. A centering. A prayer. A breath.

Today's work culture rushes. Click into Zoom. Start agenda. Zero presence.

But presence is power.

Modern Practice Tip:

Begin team sessions with a shared ritual: silence, a quote, one breath. Not to slow things down—but to tune the team like an orchestra. Clarity and connection follow.

4. Rotating Leadership Roles

In the villages of India, the panchayat didn't always have one fixed head. Leadership often rotated. Even today, in tribal councils or spiritual communities, different members take turns to lead. Why?

Because perspective shifts everything. When the listener becomes the leader, empathy grows.

In one innovation sprint I facilitated, we assigned the *most junior person* to be the final decision-maker for the day. At first, people were confused. But by lunch, the room calmed and were no longer bewildered. They were listening differently. And she rose—more confident, clearer than ever. The team rallied behind her because she had no ego.

We started doing this more often. Not to patronize, but to practice *decentralized brilliance*.

Hinduism never idolized one form of power. The Trimurti—Brahma, Vishnu, Shiva—share cosmic roles. Even Devi rotates: fierce Kali, nurturing Lakshmi, wise Saraswati. Power is fluid, not fixed.

Modern Practice Tip:

Switch roles. Let different team members run the meeting, decide the roadmap, or lead retrospectives. It's not chaos—it's consciousness.

5. Mix Elders and Young Minds

You've probably heard about the Gurukul system—students lived with gurus, not just for lessons but for *life*. But what's fascinating is how often you'd find a blend of ages in those spaces. The young would listen, but also question. The elders would guide, but also learn.

There's a story of Ashtavakra, a young boy with a crooked body but a brilliant mind. He defeats seasoned scholars in debate and becomes a sage before hitting adulthood.

Today's workplaces love to bucket people: "senior," "junior," "new hire." But real innovation emerges when age becomes an asset, not a divider.

At a large manufacturing company in Gujarat, a division struggling with declining product relevance launched a bold internal initiative. They created "Innovation Tandems," pairing every retiring employee with a new intern for 30 days. No KPIs—just observation, conversation, and co-creation. One pair—a 21-year-old engineering student and a 59-year-old floor technician—ended up designing a low-cost calibration device using old machine parts and a 3D-printed casing. The student brought fresh modeling skills; the elder brought intuition no text book could teach. Their prototype was later adopted in five production units, saving lakhs in downtime. But more than that, it sparked a cultural shift—elders felt valued again, and young minds felt empowered.

Modern Practice Tip:

Don't just mix skillsets—mix *ages*. Design innovation labs where a 23-year-old sits next to a 53-year-old. Wisdom meets fire. Gold.

6. Festivals as Team-Building Metaphors

Let's get festive for a minute.

Ever celebrated Holi with your team? One midsize design agency in Jaipur did—minus the actual colors. They hosted an “Ideathon Holi,” where the only rule was: no filters, no hierarchies, just wild ideas. Each team had to "splash" the board with concepts that were bold, absurd, or seemingly impossible. Someone suggested an app that uses scent as a UX trigger; another pitched biodegradable fashion that blooms into plants after wear. Instead of dismissing the outrageous, the group had to find one small element worth building on. For two hours, laughter mixed with post-its, and by the end, they had five new prototypes. The event didn’t just unlock creativity—it dissolved office egos. Everyone left feeling seen, and oddly, lighter.

That’s when the leadership team realized—festivals are innovation frameworks in disguise.

Holi is about playful disruption—great for creative chaos. Diwali? It’s about illumination—perfect for clarity and reflection. Navaratri? Nine days of resilience—ideal for long-haul sprints and battles of will. And Sankranti? A moment of realignment with celestial truth—perfect for team retrospectives and pivot points.

Hindu festivals aren’t just celebrations. They are cultural design tools. And if you bring that metaphor into the workplace, something shifts.

It’s not just “team bonding.” It’s story-powered collaboration. It's how emotion meets structure.

Modern Practice Tip:

Map your project phases to festival energies. Launch with Holi (creative burst), analyze with Diwali (clarity), push through with Navaratri (resilience). Bonus? Your team won't forget it.

7. Chant-Based Brainstorming

This one might sound out there—but stay with me.

Have you ever joined a kirtan or a group chant session? At first, it's awkward. But a few repetitions in, something takes over. The brain calms. The group synchronizes. You stop thinking and start *feeling*.

That's the power of rhythm.

In ancient India, chanting mantras like "Om" or "Shanti" wasn't just spiritual—it was cognitive. It entrained brainwaves, synchronized breath, and built group coherence. This wasn't accidental—it was neurological design.

At an animation studio in Chennai, a team experimenting with "nonlinear ideation" began each storyboarding session with a rhythmic drumming track in the background. Then they tried something bold: each participant had to speak one concept per beat, in a circle, no interruptions, no pauses. At first, it felt forced. But by round three, the energy flipped. Words flowed, themes emerged, and disparate ideas started connecting. A shy background artist shouted out a plot twist that became central to their next film. They called it "story kirtan." The format stuck—every major campaign since then has begun with rhythm-based idea rounds. It wasn't about music. It was about flow.

Think of it like innovation jazz, or raaga.

Modern Practice Tip:

Use rhythm—literally. Try rhythmic speaking rounds. Play loops while ideating. Or just chant together. Sounds silly? So did brainstorming once.

8. Adopt Seva Culture

The first time I experienced seva was at a Langar in a Sikh gurdwara. No one asked for credit. Everyone served. CEOs wiped floors next to cab drivers. It was humbling—and strangely empowering.

In Hindu traditions, seva is selfless service—no ego, no credit-hunting. In Bhakti Yoga, it's how you dissolve the self. In Karma Yoga, it's how you align duty with divinity.

Now, what does that mean in the workplace?

At a tech nonprofit in Bengaluru preparing for a major donor demo, disaster struck—half the dev team came down with viral fever. With the launch deadline two days away, roles blurred. A marketing intern jumped in to format data dashboards. The office admin helped test logins on mobile browsers. A backend engineer quietly designed the presentation slides. No one was assigned anything—they just flowed toward the need. After the demo (which went flawlessly), there were no medals or emails of praise. Just a quiet moment where someone brought chai for the whole team and said, "We pulled a miracle, together." That week, no one burned out. They burned brighter.

When teams adopt seva, collaboration becomes sacred. There's less "mine vs. yours," more "ours." Innovation stops being a race and becomes a gift.

Modern Practice Tip:

Set up peer support pods. Encourage teammates to help outside roles. Celebrate silent helpers. Kill the ego, grow the outcome.

9. Gurukul-Style Co-Living Sessions

Co-living sounds like a hippie thing, right? But think again.

In the Gurukul, students didn't just learn from books—they lived with the guru. They absorbed dharma through observation. They learned ethics over meals, resilience through chores, and creativity through nature.

A tech accelerator in Colorado, USA once tried an unconventional experiment for its newest startup cohort. Instead of hotel rooms and scheduled workshops, they housed ten founders in a renovated farmhouse for two weeks. No formal agenda—just shared responsibilities. Breakfasts were cooked in rotation, evenings ended around a fire pit, and cleaning duties were randomly assigned. What emerged wasn't just camaraderie—it was creative combustion. A fintech founder struggling with user onboarding ended up reimagining his interface after a midnight dishwashing debate with a UX expert from a health startup. A solo founder known for staying guarded opened up about burnout while chopping vegetables, which led to three others designing a self-care tracker as a side project.

There were no name tags. No pitch decks. Just humans building trust through shared living. It was a crash course in empathy, friction, and flow. And long after the retreat ended, many of those partnerships outlasted the startups themselves.

In a world of remote work, that kind of real-time trust is rare. But once built, it lasts.

Modern Practice Tip:

Host innovation retreats. Stay under one roof. Cook together. Play. Learn. Watch what surfaces when the "workspace" becomes life.

10. Shared Metaphor-Building

Let me leave you with a powerful tool that's often ignored—shared metaphors.

In the Rigveda, there's a beautiful hymn called the *Purusha Sukta*. It describes the cosmos as a divine being—where each organ, each limb has a role. The mouth becomes Brahmins (speech), arms become Kshatriyas (strength), thighs become Vaishyas (support), feet become Shudras (foundation). It's not hierarchy—it's harmony.

Now imagine this metaphor applied to teams. At a creative agency in Toronto, Canada working on a complex global campaign, team dynamics were quietly breaking down. Designers felt overruled by strategy leads. Project managers felt unseen. Deadlines were slipping. A facilitator came in—not with a gantt chart, but with a giant blank canvas. “If this project were a machine,” she asked, “what part are you?” A copywriter said, “I’m the spark plug—tiny, but I start the fire.” A client liaison added, “I think I’m the suspension system—I absorb shocks from the outside.” Laughter broke the tension. What followed was a visual group mapping—gears, levers, wires—all drawn out, with sticky notes naming each role. In two hours, the team didn’t just feel heard—they felt part of something cohesive. Deadlocks eased. Collaboration reawakened. Shared metaphors create shared meaning. And in innovation, meaning is glue.

Modern Practice Tip:

Use metaphor mapping. Build team identity through symbols. Give shared purpose a name—“this is our Kurukshetra moment” or “our tapasya phase.” Story makes strategy stick.

Conclusion:

Collaboration as a Catalyst for Innovation

If there’s one thing I hope you take away from this chapter, it’s this: collaboration is more than just team meetings and project plans. It's a *spiritual design choice*.

When you open space for every voice, you’re not just being inclusive—you’re accessing *collective intelligence*.

When you adopt rituals, festivals, chants, or metaphorical language in your team, you're not being "soft." You're tuning the frequency for flow, trust, and breakthrough ideas. When you bring in people who don't look, think, or work like you, you're not adding friction—you're expanding your horizon.

Our dharmic ancestors understood this. They built innovation not in silos but in sanghas, not in pyramids but in circles. They invited the strange, the divine, the outcast, and the wise—all into one space. Why? Because innovation thrives at the edges—of thought, culture, age, and tradition.

In the AI age, the most human thing you can do is collaborate deeply. Machines can process. They can optimize. But only humans can *co-create meaning*. That's our edge.

So, as you lead your teams into the future, take a bit of Janaka's sabha with you. Light a diya before a brainstorm. Rotate leadership. Mix generations. Chant out your wildest ideas. Let your teams become temples—where something higher shows up when you truly create together.

Because when collaboration becomes sacred, innovation becomes unstoppable.

Chapter - 3

Customer Centricity

Sacred Service: Building with The Heart of The User

Introduction: Walking the Path of Empathy in Innovation

Innovation isn't born in boardrooms; it's born in the marketplace, on the streets, in the quiet corners where people live, struggle, dream, and grow. In this chapter, we shift our lens from technologies and tools to the sacred heart of innovation: the customer. In the Hindu tradition, the idea of the 'seeker' is revered—but what if in the modern business world, the customer is the seeker and the sacred teacher all at once?

The saints of India never lived apart from the people. They walked among them, heard their stories, and spoke their language. In doing so, they embodied a profound form of empathy and humility that today's brands can learn from. In this chapter, we explore ten powerful ways customer-centricity can become not just a strategy, but a dharmic practice. From treating feedback as sacred to honoring life events and giving prasadam, these practices draw from the wellsprings of Indian wisdom to show us how to lead with soul.

Whether you're building an AI product or a small family business, these ideas invite you to slow down, bow down, and truly see your customer—not as a target or metric, but as a co-creator of your innovation journey

1. Empathy Walks Through Communities

Back in the 15th century, Kabir, the weaver-saint, and Mirabai, the wandering bhakta of Krishna, didn't just sit in temples philosophizing. They walked. They lived with potters, weavers, cobblers. They heard the songs of the streets and slept under open skies with farmers. It wasn't charity. It was immersion. Real life, raw and truthful.

A few years ago, a team at a Canadian urban planning startup was trying to create a mobile solution for public transport payment in underserved neighborhoods. Their app looked perfect on paper—QR-enabled, multi-modal, subsidy tracking. But usage lagged. So they decided to ditch the office for a week and embed with local bus commuters in Toronto's inner suburbs. They stood in line at dawn bus stops, rode packed rush-hour routes, and visited the corner stores where people topped up their cards. That's when they noticed something: most users avoided scanning anything digital out of fear they'd be tracked by immigration or government authorities. The solution wasn't tech—it was trust. They pivoted to anonymous reload tokens and saw usage spike. That never came from data. It came from walking.

Walking through communities doesn't just mean physically being there. It's about *absorbing*, observing, asking without ego. You can feel when someone has done it. Their product feels... human.

Innovation isn't just algorithms and brainstorms in whiteboard rooms. It's forged in the field, on dusty roads, in chai stalls, in overheard conversations. It's tactile, not just digital.

If your business sells to humans, it must *know* humans—not via metrics, but moments. And no spreadsheet can show you the heartbreak of a late paycheck like a conversation can.

Modern Practice Tip:

Every quarter, do an 'Empathy Walk'. Go into a customer's world. No suits. No pitch. Just presence. Reflect, then redesign.

2. User Testing as Darshan

In temples, darshan isn't just you seeing the deity. The deity sees *you* back. It's not one-way. It's a sacred exchange. That's the spirit we need in user testing.

Too many companies treat user testing like a formality. "Here's our product. What do you think?" But real innovation starts when we let the customer *change* us. When we see them, and allow ourselves to be seen.

Based in Singapore, a startup designing a financial literacy app for rural women kept hitting a wall. Their UX team had run dozens of surveys and digital usability tests, but app usage was stagnant. A local advisor suggested something different: hold in-person sessions at community prayer halls where these women gathered weekly. The team set up a space with tea and stools, no screens, just conversations. One quiet grandmother pointed to the cartoon avatars in the app and said softly, "I don't trust them—they look like they're watching me." That single comment unlocked the insight they'd missed for months. The avatars were too animated, too polished—they triggered discomfort, not confidence.

The team redesigned the interface to feature real community voices, audio stories, and visuals that resembled sari-clad local mentors. They even added a button that said *"Ask Like a Sister"*. Adoption surged. Not because of better wireframes, but because of deeper *darshan*—mutual seeing, mutual transformation.

Customer interaction isn't checkbox testing. It's *darshan*. The moment where the divine within the user reflects the divine within the product team.

Modern Practice Tip:

Make user feedback sessions ritualistic. Light incense if you must. Frame them as mutual transformation events. Don't just gather data—be changed.

3. Create Avatars of Customers

Vishnu didn't just stay in one form. He became fish, turtle, lion-man, prince, teacher—evolving as society needed. Our customers evolve, too.

A mobile learning company based in Vietnam was initially designing courses for garment factory workers in the Mekong Delta. Their user persona was flat: "Female, age 30, limited literacy." It made development easy—but impact stayed low. So, a team member proposed an unusual approach inspired by Buddhist storytelling traditions. They created evolving life avatars instead of static personas: "Lan, the Silent Learner" became "Lan the Aspiring Trader" as she started dreaming of selling on Facebook. Then she grew into "Lan the Mentor," helping new factory recruits navigate the system. Each version of Lan had different motivations, fears, and needs.

By developing this storyline, the product team realized their app couldn't just teach reading—it needed modules on micro-entrepreneurship, audio-guided interfaces, and peer learning tools. What started as one persona became a multidimensional journey. And user engagement jumped—because the product was growing *with* the user.

By embodying avatars, we develop *longitudinal empathy*— not just who users are now, but who they will become. This is crucial in AI-led products, where learning loops must mirror real human growth.

Modern Practice Tip:

Build customer avatars not just as snapshots but storylines. Map their evolution. Ask: what form must we take to serve their next stage?

4. Celebrate Feedback as Sacred

Hindu families often bless a child who dares to speak truth to elders. That's because critique, in the right spirit, is sacred.

In Manila, a Filipino e-commerce startup was preparing to roll out a premium delivery subscription. During a community feedback session in Quezon City, a soft-spoken single mother raised her hand. She calmly but firmly said, "You're charging for speed—but your drivers often miss the window. If you can't deliver dignity, don't sell convenience." The room fell silent. Some team members bristled. But the CEO stood up, bowed slightly, and said, "That feedback is our mirror. Thank you." The next day, the team brought that customer into a working session. They restructured their delivery promise and added real-time customer chat—features inspired directly by her. Months later, she not only renewed her subscription but started referring others through a testimonial video she volunteered to make.

That critic? She became our most loyal ambassador.

Treat feedback not as friction, but as devotion. Someone cared enough to point out a flaw. That is grace.

This attitude creates safety. People open up. And when they do, real insight flows.

Modern Practice Tip:

Celebrate customer feedback. Publicly. Give shoutouts, gifts, or even digital badges. It signals that you *honour* their voice.

5. Use Panchatantra-Style Stories

The Panchatantra didn't use PowerPoint. It used talking animals. A monkey teaches loyalty. A crocodile warns of betrayal. Why? Because stories bypass ego. They hit the heart.

At a railway technology startup in Ahmedabad, the team was tasked with improving elderly passenger onboarding. The engineers came armed with spreadsheets—wait times, stair counts, escalator speeds. But nothing moved the operations team. Then a junior UX researcher rewrote the problem as a *Panchatantra*-style fable: "Dadaji the Elephant arrives at the station. He must cross the forest (platform stairs), avoid the rushing monkeys (crowds), and reach the mango tree (his train) before sunset.

But his knees are old, and the jackal at the help desk is too busy…" The room burst out laughing—but then, quietly, heads nodded. Within a week, they piloted a red-jacket "Squirrel Squad" to escort elderly passengers. The story became legend in the office. That tale moved more hearts than any chart ever could.

Metaphor is memory's best friend. If you want people to care about a customer pain point, *narrate* it. Dress it in animal skin. Make it feel ancient and wise.

Modern Practice Tip:

Convert your customer journey maps into short stories. Share them in meetings. Bonus: Use archetypes like clever foxes or wise elephants.

6. Map Customer Karma Paths

In the Gita, Krishna explains karma: every action has consequences. Invisible threads link cause and effect. Customer experience is like that.

Every touchpoint—an email, a tone, a delay—creates karmic residue. Done right, it builds trust. Done poorly, it haunts.

In Thailand, a mobility startup offering bike and scooter rentals noticed a drop in renewals. On investigation, it wasn't price or performance—it was one forgotten email. Users who paused their subscription weren't acknowledged. One customer even wrote, "I left quietly.

You didn't notice." That struck a chord. The team created an "Offboarding Blessing"—a goodbye email with a thank-you note and a curated map of biking trails near the user's last location. One customer shared it in a local Facebook group, calling it "the first breakup that felt like closure." That post led to a ripple of goodwill and a wave of returning users months later.

It wasn't a retention strategy—it was karmic repair.

Don't just fix problems. Heal relationships. Build positive emotional karma.

Modern Practice Tip:

Map your customer journey like a karmic loop. List actions, reactions, emotional residues. Aim to leave every touchpoint better than you found it.

7. Ritualize User Interviews

In the Upanishads, students begin by bowing. Then comes curiosity. Then listening. Then dialogue.

When you treat user interviews as rituals, the energy shifts. The user isn't a subject. They're a teacher. A guru.

In Jerusalem, a civic-tech startup building digital tools for municipal services found their interviews were falling flat. Users were polite, but guarded. So a researcher with a background in Jewish philosophy suggested a shift: begin each interview with a moment of gratitude—thanking the user not for their time, but for their lived experience. Then, before the first question, they recited a version of the Hebrew blessing *"Baruch atah...*

shehecheyanu," rephrased to honour the moment of shared learning. The change was subtle but profound. One elderly resident teared up, saying, "No one's ever thanked me just for living through the system." What followed was a flood of stories—frustrations, insights, small wins—that no survey could have unearthed.

Those interviews didn't just gather data. They built reverence. And that reverence translated into better design, rooted in dignity.

This energy cannot be faked. Rituals elevate conversation. They remind us: the user is not a number, they are a soul.

Modern Practice Tip:

Begin interviews with an intention. End with a reflection. This isn't New Age fluff. It's ancient UX design.

8. Celebrate Customer Life Events

Temples remember their devotees. They know your birthday. They bless your anniversary. That's not CRM. That's memory with love.

Modern brands have the tools. But the spirit? That's rare.

In Ohio (USA), a regional credit union wanted to build stronger relationships with its aging members. Instead of relying solely on automated birthday emails, they launched a program called "Living Legacy." A customer service rep handpicked a few long-time members each month and mailed a printed photo collage from their first year of membership—if available—along with a personal letter. One woman in her 90s received a copy of her original account application from 1968, along with a note that read, "You've been part of our story for over 50 years.

Thank you for letting us be part of yours." Her grandson shared it on social media, calling it "the first piece of mail that made Grandma cry—in a good way."

These moments build bonds no chatbot can replace.

Don't just *track* customer events. Honour them. Celebrate them.

Modern Practice Tip:

Create a calendar of key customer life events. Automate what you can, but add one human touch. A voice note. A photo. A prayer.

9. Cross-Class Empathy Sessions

Ravidas was a leatherworker. He spoke truths that shook kings. Because he *knew* suffering. Real insight often comes from below.

At a national grocery chain in the U.S., the corporate design team was struggling to improve an employee scheduling tool. Endless feedback loops with managers led to only marginal improvements. Then someone proposed a cross-role empathy session—not with store supervisors, but with the night shift crew: shelf stockers, janitors, and early morning inventory checkers. The session was hosted in the breakroom of a small-town store in Missouri. There, a 62-year-old overnight worker quietly explained how the current app kept defaulting to shifts that clashed with her dialysis schedule. Another, a single father, shared how swapping shifts meant driving across town just to log into a store computer—costing him gas he couldn't afford. These stories didn't just reshape the UI—they reframed the mission. The team added mobile access, a shift-swap feature, and empathetic messaging.

It's easy to innovate for people like you. It's powerful to innovate for people who have no voice in your boardroom.

Invite them in.

Modern Practice Tip:

Once a quarter, host an empathy circle with your lowest-paid workers. Let them share stories. Thank them. Design with their truths in mind.

10. Offer Customer Prasadam

Prasadam is sacred food. A token. A gesture. After darshan, you get it in your palm. You feel seen.

Brands send gifts. But they're often transactional. True prasadam is thoughtful.

A conceptual example: Imagine a rising ed-tech startup based in Coimbatore that wanted to honour its earliest rural school users. Instead of sending slick merchandise or discount coupons, they crafted a different offering. Each school received a parcel containing a small packet of native basil seeds (Tulasi), symbolic of nourishment and reverence in Hindu households, along with a soft palm-leaf bookmark etched with the phrase *“Seva hi Shiksha hai”*—Service is Learning. Included was a message printed in both Tamil and English: *“This is not a gift. It’s our gratitude, planted.”* One teacher wrote back saying she’d planted the seeds with her students as part of a classroom ritual. Another framed the bookmark near her attendance register.

The cost? Less than a cup of coffee (or chai). But the gesture created something far richer than brand recall—it seeded trust, reverence, and continuity.

You don’t need big budgets to be sacred. Just sincerity.

Modern Practice Tip:

Create a "prasadam" practice. Design small, meaningful gifts. Not bribes. Blessings. Let them say: we see you. We thank you.

Conclusion

Customer-centricity in the age of AI doesn’t mean just knowing what your users click on. It means remembering their name, honoring their story, and acknowledging their sacred place in your journey. Every design decision, every feedback loop, every line of code must carry this energy: reverence.

These ten ideas aren’t hacks. They’re habits. Cultural mindsets. Dharmic blueprints for building businesses that care deeply and authentically. When we root our innovation in the real lives of customers—not just as consumers but as co-travelers—we access deeper intuition, greater trust, and longer-lasting impact.

In a world obsessed with speed and scale, this chapter invites you to pause, connect, and innovate with heart. Because in honoring the customer, you honor the very purpose of your enterprise. That is the path of dharma-driven innovation.

Chapter - 4

Risk Is The Engine Of Innovation

Courageous Leaps Through Dharma and Design

Introduction: Where Fear Meets Dharma, Innovation Begins

Risk is the heartbeat of innovation. It's the space between what you know and what you dare to believe is possible. But in most corporate cultures, risk has become synonymous with recklessness, or worse—career suicide. That's why so many smart people build safe things. They stay in their lanes. They ship incrementally. And in doing so, they starve their deepest genius.

But Hindu tradition sees risk differently. From Hanuman's leap to Aryabhata's cosmic recalibrations, risk is not the enemy—it's the initiator. Risk is tapasya, the fire that tests your resolve and reveals your power. It's where Dharma—your true role—emerges.

Ancient Indian epics, sciences, and philosophies weren't built in comfort zones. They were born from exile, failure, rebellion, and questioning the unthinkable. That's exactly what today's AI-driven world needs. Not more safety. But more wisdom in the face of risk.

In this chapter, we dive into ten powerful practices inspired by Hindu stories and sages that help modern teams build a **culture of intelligent risk-taking**. You'll learn how to reward effort, not just outcome. How to use play, not pressure. How to document failure as sacred learning. And how to tackle the taboos no one wants to name.

Because the future isn't built by the fearless. It's built by the brave.

1. "Safe to Fail" Experiments

In the Ramayana, when Hanuman was asked to leap across the ocean to Lanka, he didn't yet know he could fly. He had forgotten his powers. It was only in mid-leap, trusting his purpose, that his abilities returned to him. His greatness didn't precede the leap—it emerged from it.

There's something poetic about leaping before you're ready. In modern business, especially with AI, we often want to calculate every outcome before even attempting a bold move. But some truths are only discovered in motion. A small internal pilot, an unbranded test, or a sandbox trial—these are our Lanka leaps. And like Hanuman, we often remember our hidden strength not in planning rooms, but in midair.

The key here is not about gambling recklessly, but about designing "safe-to-fail" environments. These are controlled experiments where failure is not only expected—it's invited. It's where teams feel free to try things outside the norm, to question what the data can't explain yet.

When you allow failure without punishment, you create space for growth. It's in that safety that boldness takes root. The lesson from Hanuman is that courage is not the absence of fear—it's the willingness to act before proof.

Think about AI implementations. Not everything will be successful on the first try. You may build a chatbot that doesn't convert. Or launch an automation that backfires. But if you've designed the sandbox well, you've lost nothing—and gained immense insight.

Let your team leap. And remind them: their wings may find them in the air.

Modern Practice Tip:

Design quarterly "safe-to-fail" experiments where teams can pitch and test an idea that may not work. No KPIs. No ROI. Just potential. Debrief what was learned—especially if it failed.

2. Wall of Failed Ideas (Lessons Learned)

Ancient Ayurvedic texts like the Charaka Samhita and Sushruta Samhita are not just filled with remedies—they're filled with failed experiments. Mistakes were meticulously documented so future vaidyas wouldn't repeat them. In Hindu tradition, failure wasn't shameful—it was scholarly.

Fast-forward to today's corporate world, and we do the opposite. We bury our failed campaigns, erase failed product launches from our resumes, and pretend the detour never happened. But in a culture of innovation, failure is sacred data.

Imagine a wall—yes, an actual wall—where every failed idea is posted proudly, along with what was learned. Think of it as a "Wisdom from Failure" wall. Not to mock, but to memorialize. Because what failed in one season may become brilliant in another.

If an idea didn't work, great. What did you learn about your audience? Your technology? Your assumptions? Make that insight visible to others. Future teams shouldn't start at zero. Let them stand on your broken prototypes.

Just like Ayurveda evolved by preserving what didn't work, your organization evolves by preserving the "near-misses" and "almost-there" ideas.

When teams see that even the best fail—and that failure is documented, respected, and used—they stop hiding their boldness. They become learners.

Modern Practice Tip:

Build a "Wall of Learning" where failed ideas are logged with what was learned. Celebrate contributions to this wall during town halls or retrospectives.

3. Invite Bold Outsiders to Critique

In the Mahabharata, it wasn't a Pandava who led them to victory—it was Krishna, an outsider to the Kuru bloodline. Sometimes, clarity comes from those outside the echo chamber.

Modern companies, especially tech-driven ones, love expertise. But the downside of expertise is groupthink. Everyone knows too much of the same thing. Innovation, on the other hand, often comes from the edge—from the artist, the skeptic, the customer, or even the child.

You've built your product for six months. You're proud. But when a poet or a 12-year-old tests it and says, "Why is it so complicated?"—you might uncover gold.

Outsiders ask strange questions. They challenge sacred cows. They don't care how long it took to build the feature. They just want it to make sense. That's powerful.

Krishna never fought directly, but his insights shifted the course of war. Invite your own Krishnas. Bring in people who don't "fit." Let the data scientist meet the dancer. Let your compliance officer hear from a comedian.

And then listen. Deeply. Because these perspectives may be the one thing that saves your product—or reveals your next one.

Modern Practice Tip:

Once per quarter, host an "Outsider Review Day" where non-team members give raw feedback. Include artists, students, activists, or even retired customers.

4. Lanka Leap Day

Hanuman's leap to Lanka wasn't just an act of strength—it was an act of radical belief. The Vanaras didn't know if such a leap was possible. No one had done it. But belief stretched into reality because someone dared.

Innovation thrives when we make space for the impossible. But in our boardrooms, everything is filtered through feasibility. ROI. Resource bandwidth. Approval gates. In that environment, no one even dreams about the outlandish.

What if you institutionalized a day where the only ideas allowed were the ones that *shouldn't* work? No business case. No market validation. Just raw belief and vision. That's Lanka Leap Day.

On Lanka Leap Day, pitch the impossible. A product no one's asking for. A feature that defies current tech limits.

A collaboration with a competitor. Even an idea that has "0% feasibility today" written on the first slide. The point isn't to launch it—it's to stretch.

Stretching belief doesn't mean you go launch every idea. It means you learn to think beyond today's limits. Some of these leaps, while wild now, may become doable later as tech advances or AI evolves.

And sometimes, the idea may not be so wild after all. The first web browser, cloud computing, even smart speakers—they all started as Lanka Leaps. Too risky, too expensive, too early. Until someone leapt.

Modern Practice Tip:

Host a quarterly "Lanka Leap Day" where wild, currently unviable ideas are pitched with full creative flair. Encourage moonshot thinking, and reward the most imaginative—not the most realistic.

5. Celebrate Risky Efforts, Not Just Wins

Bhagiratha's story is legendary. He attempted to bring the celestial river Ganga to Earth, an act of immense difficulty. He failed many times. But his repeated efforts moved the gods, and he became immortal in memory. Even today, Ganga is called "Bhagirathi" in his honor—not because he succeeded easily, but because he *tried relentlessly*.

Our corporate world tends to worship results. Did it win? Did it go viral? Did it make money? But innovation often doesn't work like that. The most crucial attempts may not bear fruit in the quarter you want them to. Some efforts plant seeds.

Bhagiratha Awards—that's what you need. Recognize those who took the riskiest swings, who ventured where others hesitated, even if they didn't "win." That recognition tells your team: we value courage as much as we value outcome.

When you praise effort, you build a courageous culture. And courageous cultures *try more*. Over time, that increases innovation velocity dramatically.

And even more importantly, it creates psychological safety. People don't shrink from bold ideas out of fear of embarrassment. They step up, knowing even if they fail, they'll be honored like Bhagiratha—for trying what others didn't dare.

Modern Practice Tip:

Establish an internal "Bhagiratha Award" to honor the boldest, most meaningful failure or near-miss each quarter. Focus on learning, ambition, and resilience.

6. Challenge Truths like Aryabhata

Aryabhata, the great Indian mathematician and astronomer, dared to suggest the Earth rotated on its axis—a view considered laughable or even heretical in his time. Yet, he persisted with clarity, humility, and rigorous logic. He didn't destroy old truths—he refined them.

Risk in innovation doesn't always look like a new feature. Sometimes, it's questioning a fundamental assumption. Is this process necessary? Is this belief even valid today? These are the kinds of questions that birth paradigm shifts.

In your workplace, you need Aryabhata moments. Sessions where someone can say: “What if we’re wrong?” And not get shut down.

Respectful rebellion—that’s the key. Question, but with sincerity. Propose alternatives backed by logic. Make “constructive defiance” a virtue, not a vice.

Aryabhata didn’t have social media to defend himself. He had courage and data. You have both—and a team. Use them.

Modern Practice Tip:

Hold monthly “What If We’re Wrong?” sessions where teams challenge long-held assumptions and outdated KPIs. Ask: If we had to do this from scratch today, would we do it the same way?

7. Keep a Risk Diary

Yogis have long kept journals—not of external activity, but of internal shifts. Their fears, breakthroughs, temptations, and detours were all logged with care. It wasn’t narcissism—it was awareness training. Knowing the self makes one wiser in the face of risk.

Now imagine applying that to corporate life. Every product manager, every designer, every marketer—keeping a personal “risk journal.” A log of what scared them, what bold move they made that day, and what they learned.

It's not just documentation—it's therapy. Most fear is vague and emotional. But when you write it down— "I feared launching without approval," or "I avoided pitching my idea to leadership"—you start noticing patterns.

Over time, your risk muscle strengthens. You become self-aware. And that makes your risks smarter, not smaller.

Companies often look for risk-tolerant people. But here's a secret: Risk tolerance isn't a personality trait—it's a practice. A habit. A reflection routine.

Start journaling your boldness, and watch it grow.

Modern Practice Tip:

Encourage team members to keep weekly "Risk Journals" where they log one risk they took, one fear they felt, and one lesson they gained. Offer optional sharing in retros or huddles.

8. Gamify Exploration

Games like *Chaturanga*—the ancestor of chess—weren't just for amusement. They trained minds in strategy, morality, and patience. Even war stories in the Mahabharata used dice games and riddles to explore deeper themes. In Dharmic traditions, play is a gateway to wisdom.

Modern innovation teams often suffer from seriousness fatigue. Everything is a deliverable. Every idea needs a roadmap. But creativity doesn't flourish under constant pressure—it thrives in play.

Gamification isn't just for customers—it's for creators. Turn exploration into a game. Award points for ideas pitched, risks taken, or even weird prototypes attempted.

Make it fun. Let teams earn "explorer" badges or win goofy trophies. Create internal quests—like "Pitch something no one asked for" or "Revive a failed concept from 2019."

When exploration becomes play, resistance disappears. People volunteer. They laugh. And in that laughter, incredible ideas are born.

Modern Practice Tip:

Turn risk-taking into a game with points, achievements, or creative quests. Offer playful rewards—like "Best Wild Idea," "Explorer of the Month," or "Chaos Champ."

9. Worst-Case Scenarios

The exile of the Pandavas wasn't just tragic—it was a result of underestimating betrayal. The dice game wasn't just risky—it was poorly prepared. What if they had game-planned for the worst-case?

Risk doesn't mean ignoring failure. It means preparing for it. Thinking it through. Designing buffers.

One of the best innovation tools? Scenario planning. Not just the best-case and base-case—but the ugly, painful, humiliating worst-case. What if the customer hates it?

What if the tech breaks? What if our lead developer leaves?

Once you've named your fears, they shrink. And when you plan for them, they often don't happen.

Worst-case simulations aren't pessimistic—they're smart. And they make bold action feel safer, because you've visualized the bottom.

Ironically, it's those who imagine failure who end up with the fewest surprises.

Modern Practice Tip:

Run quarterly "Doom Drills" where teams imagine and prepare for the worst-case scenario of their boldest initiative. Practice recovery strategies in advance.

10. Reverse Hackathons

Ancient Indian sages didn't shy away from hard questions. In fact, Upanishadic teaching often began with the student asking: "What is the meaning of death? Who am I?" These were not easy inquiries—but they were welcomed.

In corporate life, we avoid the hard problems. The legacy systems no one wants to touch. The culture issue everyone sidesteps. The ethical dilemma hidden under AI training data. But these "untouchables" are often the ripest for innovation.

Reverse hackathons flip the script. Instead of solving the obvious, you ask teams to tackle the things no one wants to admit exist. The politically sensitive issues. The inconvenient truths.

Set aside a day. Bring brave minds together. Frame the issue carefully. And then… explore. No judgment. Just inquiry and prototypes.

You'll be amazed. Often, the biggest breakthroughs come from the problems we buried the deepest.

Modern Practice Tip:

Host biannual "Reverse Hackathons" where teams work on taboo, ignored, or unpopular problems—like burnout, ethics, or broken internal systems.

Conclusion Summary Turning Dharma into Daring

If there's one thing the Mahabharata, the Ramayana, the Vedas, and the Upanishads all agree on, it's this: the path of purpose will always require risk. But it's not random risk. It's not gambling. It's **purposeful experimentation**, where even the missteps carry meaning.

In today's world of artificial intelligence and exponential change, the biggest risk is playing it safe. The companies that will lead tomorrow are the ones who ask hard questions today, who invite critiques, who document their stumbles and turn them into stepping stones.

Hanuman didn't know he could fly. Bhagiratha didn't know if Ganga would descend. Aryabhata didn't know if he'd be believed. But they acted. They documented. They tried again. And because of that, they shifted reality.

Now it's your turn.

As you build AI tools, launch products, challenge systems, or rethink your career, use these ten frameworks to test your edge. Turn risk into ritual. Turn failures into fuel. And above all, build a culture where people feel safe to be bold.

Because innovation isn't just the destination. It's how courage dances with uncertainty—again and again, until something timeless is born.

Chapter - 5

Leadership Support

Water the Roots, Not Just the Fruits: How Ancient Trust Models Unlock Modern Innovation

Introduction: The Sacred Fuel Behind Innovation

Every startup dreams of building a rocket ship. But too many forget to fill the tank. That fuel? It's not capital, not even talent—it's leadership support. Innovation doesn't survive on permission alone. It needs protection. It needs belief. It needs the kind of nurturing that Hindu tradition encoded deep into its stories, epics, and cultural rhythms.

If you study ancient Indian wisdom, you'll see a fascinating pattern: the most legendary acts of creation, transformation, and breakthrough didn't happen in isolation. They happened under the watchful eyes—and open arms—of leaders who *chose* to support what they didn't always understand. Kings backed wandering sages. Gods backed curious warriors. Philosophers backed rebellious students. Because support wasn't about control. It was about *faith in the potential of others*.

In today's fast-paced AI-driven world, we've replaced that human faith with KPIs and dashboards. But data doesn't invent the future. People do. And people need to feel safe, seen, and supported in order to unlock their boldest work. The truth is, the next breakthrough idea in your company isn't hiding in the market—it's hiding inside someone who's waiting for your trust.

This chapter is about ten ways leaders—at every level—can return to a more *Dharmic model* of innovation support. It's not soft. It's not spiritual fluff. It's deeply practical. And if you want a team that dares, builds, questions, and creates—you'll want to learn from these ancient models that made innovation a sacred act of leadership.

1. Guru-Shishya Mentorship Sessions

In a quiet corner of the forest, a boy named Nachiketa dared to question the very meaning of life and death. He wasn't afraid—despite the fact that his "mentor" was none other than Yama, the god of death himself. This was no ordinary Q&A. It was a fearless pursuit of truth. And what's remarkable is that Yama didn't dismiss him. He didn't say "you're too young" or "come back when you're qualified." Instead, Yama answered. Deeply. Patiently. And with full respect for the young seeker's curiosity.

Now jump forward 3,000 years to a glass-walled conference room in Toronto. A junior analyst is hesitating. She wants to ask her manager something that's been bothering her: *Why do we never challenge the assumption that we need to outprice our competitors?* But she doesn't. Because she's not sure if it's "appropriate" to ask those kinds of questions in a boardroom. That's the gap. That's the problem.

In ancient India, mentorship wasn't transactional. It wasn't about reviewing PowerPoints or scheduling performance reviews. It was a sacred relationship. A guru didn't just transfer skills—they helped shape worldviews. And a true shishya wasn't afraid to challenge. The guru welcomed it. Real mentorship was based on dialogue, not download.

Businesses today can learn from this model. Imagine a company where every senior leader held weekly *Guru-Shishya sessions*—not to check performance, but to allow open, fearless inquiry. What if an intern could ask the CEO about the ethics of their supply chain without fear? What if a developer could question the AI training model without being labeled difficult? You'd have a culture of insight, not just output.

A product company in Hyderabad quietly launched something inspired by this ancient mentorship dynamic. Instead of formal reviews, they introduced *"Samvaad Circles"*—monthly in-person dialogues where juniors and seniors gathered in an open courtyard space they named *Vichar Vatika* (Garden of Thought). No laptops, no titles, no fixed agenda. A junior coder once asked the CTO, "Why do we use Western UX metaphors for rural users in Bihar?" That question sparked a full re-evaluation of the design language—resulting in localized iconography that boosted rural engagement by over 30%. Another time, a finance intern asked, "Is it ethical that we delay vendor payments to improve cash flow?" That led to an internal audit and new vendor fairness policy. What began as open-ended questioning slowly evolved into a culture of ethical innovation. The CTO later said, "We're building better software now—not just because we listen to users, but because we're finally listening to each other."

Innovation isn't always about more data. Sometimes it's about deeper conversations. The guru-shishya model proves that powerful ideas emerge not from hierarchy, but from trust. Trust to ask, to be wrong, to think deeply. In a world of AI and automation, this kind of human mentorship is more valuable than ever. Because while machines can answer, only humans can mentor.

Modern Practice Tip:

Start a monthly "Big Questions Session" at your workplace. Leaders and mentees sit in an open, non-hierarchical format. No goal but this: ask what matters. Make space for questions like "Are we proud of what we build?" or "What would we do if we weren't afraid of losing revenue?" Document the answers—and the questions. This is where innovation begins.

2. Budget for Wild Ideas

When Emperor Ashoka had his great transformation after the Kalinga war, he did something remarkable. He didn't just invest in infrastructure—he poured money into monasteries, thinkers, monks, artists, and even wandering philosophers. There was no spreadsheet ROI. Ashoka wasn't asking, "What's the quarterly return on investing in a monk?" But he did it anyway. Why? Because he understood that wild ideas need patronage, not pressure.

Now think about today's corporate budget meetings. Most line items need hard justifications—percentages, forecasts, outcomes. Try telling your CFO, "We want $100,000 for a wild idea with no defined output yet." You'll probably get laughed out of the room. But that's the very reason innovation feels so scarce—it's always filtered through KPIs.

One of the most underappreciated realities in Hindu history is that spiritual and intellectual freedom was made possible *because* it was funded. Kings like Vikramaditya didn't just tolerate eccentric scholars—they *sponsored* them. They understood that the long arc of civilizational growth bends through the imagination of a few brave misfits.

I once consulted for a mid-sized fintech in Toronto. Their CEO took a crazy step: he set up a "non-ROI discretionary innovation budget." No justification needed. Any employee could pitch a 5-minute voice note to a panel of 3 internal "guardians of the weird." They funded ideas like a video game for teaching retirement savings, an AI bot for financial journaling, and a comic book about digital fraud. Some failed. But one of them? It's now their most viral campaign ever.

The beauty of having a no-strings-attached innovation fund is this: it tells your people you trust their instincts—even when you don't yet understand them. That's how breakthroughs are born. The human imagination cannot flourish in a spreadsheet cell. It needs space, curiosity, and a little chaos.

We often think money limits creativity. The opposite is true. Lack of *unstructured* money limits it. Wild ideas aren't impractical. They're just unpredictable. And prediction is the enemy of innovation.

Modern Practice Tip:

Carve out 1–5% of your yearly budget for a "Wild Ideas Fund." Make the only requirement this: the idea must be strange, exciting, and untied to current KPIs. Let employees apply anonymously. Make it fun. Celebrate the courage to imagine—even more than the results.

3. Divine Architect Roles (Vishwakarma Model)

In the celestial realms of Hindu lore, Vishwakarma stood apart. He wasn't a king or a god of war. He was an engineer. But not just any engineer—he built Indra's palace, Ravana's flying chariot, and even the weapons of the gods. He had one sacred privilege: full autonomy. Nobody told him how to build. They only gave him the dream—and he figured out the rest.

In today's organizations, we kill our Vishwakarmas. We hire brilliant minds and then bury them in bureaucracy. Compliance forms, approval chains, weekly check-ins—until the original vision is so watered down, it's unrecognizable.

Imagine instead you gave someone total trust. "Here's the dream. Go build it. No micromanagement. Just bring it to life." That's how Apple built the original Macintosh. Steve Jobs gave a small team complete creative freedom. They called themselves "pirates." That computer changed history.

In Hindu tradition, Vishwakarma had no brand guidelines. No pre-approved templates. He was trusted to manifest brilliance. That's the kind of trust missing in most leadership models. We say we want innovation, but we don't give people the room to *own* their vision.

At a mid-sized fintech company based in Vancouver, leadership decided to try something radical. Inspired by the idea of creative autonomy, they launched what they called *"Builder's Mandate Week."* Once a quarter, top engineers, designers, and product leads were given five full working days—no stand-ups, no status reports, no executive check-ins—to pursue one initiative they believed would most benefit the user. One designer created a "quiet mode" for the app that helped neurodivergent users manage financial tasks with fewer distractions. Another backend developer rebuilt an internal dashboard that cut support ticket resolution time in half. But the real shift wasn't just in output—it was in energy. The team felt seen not as code writers, but as creators. One junior developer even said, "For the first time, I felt like Vishwakarma—building something from vision, not from spec." The leadership later noted that ideas from those weeks led to 40% of their product roadmap for the year.

Autonomy is the seed of ownership. And ownership leads to innovation. If you want Vishwakarma-level creations, you need Vishwakarma-level trust.

Modern Practice Tip:

Identify your internal builders. Create "Free Build Roles" or days—where they can pursue any product, design, or feature idea with zero oversight. Leaders should act only as sounding boards, not gatekeepers. Make it sacred space.

4. Leader Story Circles

Let me tell you a story about King Harsha. A powerful ruler, he held weekly "raj sabhas" not just for administrative matters—but to sit with sages and share his personal dilemmas. These weren't strategic war talks. These were soul talks. He'd say things like: "I am torn between justice and mercy. What would dharma want here?"

Now imagine your VP of Product saying that in your weekly team meeting: "I feel torn between scaling fast and staying ethical. I don't know the answer." That would be shocking, right? But what if it were normal?

In most companies, leaders hide their doubts. They think vulnerability is weakness. But in the epics, kings were expected to be vulnerable—in front of sages, queens, and even enemies. Why? Because vulnerability was the path to wisdom.

At a healthcare startup in Boston, the CEO launched a monthly internal ritual called "Truth Talks." It wasn't about strategy updates or investor wins—it was about leadership vulnerability. Each month, one senior leader sat with a small cross-functional team in a circle—no screens, no notes—and told a personal story of failure or moral conflict. One session featured the Head of Operations sharing how she once underpaid a vendor due to a rushed legal clause, only realizing it months later when the vendor folded. She cried while describing the regret. The team didn't mock her—they leaned in. After that, the legal team started double-checking not just for compliance, but for conscience. Another session featured the VP of Sales talking about losing a dream client because he tried to "close" instead of listening. These weren't war stories. They were soul reflections. And the shift was visible—junior staff stopped pretending. Honest feedback surged. Performance reviews became conversations, not defenses.

Innovation loves openness. When leaders model that, teams follow. If your execs only talk about wins, they create fear. But if they talk about doubts and losses, they create trust.

Remember: Krishna didn't just give Arjuna commands. He shared his own philosophy, his thoughts, even his doubts. It's not just about leading from the front—it's about leading from the heart.

Modern Practice Tip:

Host a monthly "Story Circle" where leaders share one honest story of failure, confusion, or growth. No slides. Just real talk. Let people ask questions. Make it cultural, not performative. And never record it keep it sacred.

5. Idea Funds with Internal Pitching

In ancient Indian courts, sages, artists, inventors—even ordinary citizens—could approach the king's court to present ideas. Not every proposal became policy, but the act of hearing them mattered. A traveling ascetic might propose a new temple ritual; a craftsman might explain a better irrigation wheel. The openness of the *sabha* to ideas made these empires dynamic, not just dominant.

That openness is missing in many modern workplaces. Employees often say, “I have ideas, but who would listen?” Leaders say, “Why don’t people speak up?” The answer is simple—there’s no formal *ritual* for ideas.

At a mid-sized logistics company in Indianapolis, leadership noticed a troubling pattern: innovation always came top-down. Despite frequent calls for “employee creativity,” nothing bubbled up from the front lines. So they launched what they called *“The Open Dock”*—a quarterly internal pitch forum held in the warehouse cafeteria. Anyone—from forklift drivers to accountants—could pitch an idea in 180 seconds. No slides. Just a mic, a timer, and a crowd. A rotating panel of peers and managers voted on the top three ideas, and a small internal fund of $15,000 was set aside each quarter to bring them to life.

One winning idea came from a shipping coordinator who suggested color-coded packing slips for different temperature-sensitive goods. It was so simple, yet so effective, that it reduced inventory errors by 18% and later got written into company SOPs nationwide. Another came from a payroll clerk who pitched an app to help drivers track fuel reimbursements in real time. It’s now one of the company’s most-used internal tools.

The key isn’t just money—it’s *permission*. When people are invited to pitch in a ceremonial, respectful way, they bring their best. It mirrors the old sabhas—where innovation was democratic, not elitist.

Modern Practice Tip:

Build a quarterly internal "Innovation Sabha." Give every employee a fair chance to pitch to leadership. Provide small seed funds for 3–5 winning ideas each cycle. Track results and recognize effort, not just outcomes.

6. Support Through Myth

There's a beautiful story where Vishwakarma builds something so radical, even Indra, the king of the gods, doesn't understand it. Yet Indra doesn't shut it down. He funds it. Supports it. He trusts Vishwakarma's *vision*, even without immediate clarity.

That's what modern leaders must learn. Visionaries often sound vague or wild at first. But instead of demanding full clarity upfront, great leaders say, "I believe in you. Let's see where this goes." That's not blind faith. That's visionary trust.

When Tesla launched, people mocked the idea of electric sports cars. When DeepMind proposed teaching AI to play Go, it sounded niche. But their leaders backed them. And that backing changed industries.

At a healthcare analytics startup in Texas, a junior data scientist proposed an unusual idea during a quarterly brainstorming session: instead of using their AI models solely for patient diagnostics, what if they analyzed the tone and emotional shifts in physician notes to predict caregiver fatigue? The leadership team was puzzled. It wasn't part of the product roadmap. There was no client asking for it. But the COO—who had a background in clinical work—paused and said, "I don't fully understand the mechanics, but I can tell you're onto something." She approved a micro-pilot: two weeks, one dataset, no KPIs. The results were startling. The AI detected burnout risk patterns that HR had missed for months. That project evolved into an internal wellbeing tool—and is now being spun out as a separate offering for hospital networks.

That one "yes" didn't come from full understanding. It came from leadership's ability to recognize conviction, not just clarity.

You don't have to understand every detail to support innovation. Mythical support is deeper—it's about belief in potential, not just process.

Modern Practice Tip:

Train leaders to spot early visionary behavior—even when it sounds fuzzy. Develop a "Support Without Certainty" policy: if a project has heart, traction, and creative logic, let it run a short, safe pilot—even if the full roadmap isn't clear.

7. Leaders Work Frontlines

King Janaka was known as a *rajarshi*—a royal sage. Despite being a powerful ruler, he would often till the fields himself. It wasn't PR. It was practice. He believed that leadership without touch was hollow. So he stayed grounded. Literally.

Today, we have executives who haven't spoken to a customer in months. Or VPs who couldn't use their own product if asked. That distance kills innovation. Because you can't solve a problem you don't *feel*.

At a fast-growing meal delivery startup based in North America, leadership began noticing a spike in customer churn—but the data wasn't revealing why. The CEO initiated a program called *"Ground Truth Days,"* requiring all senior leaders—CMO, CTO, Head of Ops—to spend one full shift each quarter on the frontline. This wasn't an observational tour. It meant actually packing boxes in the warehouse, riding along on deliveries, or answering support calls.

During one shift, the Head of Product fielded three back-to-back calls from frustrated customers who didn't receive allergy-safe packaging, despite checking the right box online. She realized the dropdown menu logic on the website was confusing, and even worse, warehouse staff didn't have visibility into it. Within two weeks, the workflow was redesigned. Customer complaints dropped 40%. The lesson wasn't in a dashboard—it was in the trenches.

Innovation starts where the friction is. And friction lives at the front. That's why Krishna spends time in the battlefield, not just the palace. That's why Ram wanders the forest before becoming king. Experience breeds empathy. Empathy breeds invention.

Modern Practice Tip:

Implement "Leadership Shadow Days." At least once per quarter, execs must work frontline roles: sales calls, customer support, fulfillment. Don't delegate—immerse. Follow it up with a debrief and action plan.

8. "Leader Backed This" Stories

Arjuna almost gave up. When he saw his family across the battlefield, his hands trembled. But Krishna stood beside him and said, "I am with you." That support gave Arjuna moral clarity. Not because Krishna said *what* to do, but because he said, "You're not alone."

In business, employees are often unsure if leadership has their back. That hesitation dampens boldness. People play it safe. They don't speak truth to power. They don't try weird things. But one clear sign of support can unlock massive courage.

At a Bangalore-based edtech company, the leadership team introduced a monthly ritual called *"With You, Always."* In each all-hands meeting, a senior leader would step forward to spotlight one team member who took an unconventional risk—even if it didn't work. During one session, the Head of Product shared how a junior content writer had proposed turning dry subject modules into comic-strip formats inspired by Amar Chitra Katha. The idea was initially met with skepticism. But instead of shutting it down, the VP said, "I may not fully get this yet, but I back your instinct—run a pilot."

The comic modules not only engaged students more, but also improved quiz completion rates in Tier 2 cities. The point wasn't just the success—it was that someone at the bottom of the org chart had taken a leap and knew leadership had their back. That story echoed across teams.

The next month, a QA engineer proposed gamifying bug tracking with local folklore characters—and got greenlit.

Public stories of support aren't just nice—they're tactical. They show people what's safe to try. And they remind us: Krishna didn't tell Arjuna what outcome to expect. He said, "Fight with heart. I stand with you."

Modern Practice Tip:

Add a "Leader Backed This" story to your internal newsletters or meetings. Highlight someone who took a risk. Let leadership explain *why* they stood by it. Normalize support for purpose, not just results.

9. Blind Idea Review Panels

In ancient *shastrartha* debates, ideas were judged on their logic—not on who said them. It was common for a young student to win against a royal priest if their arguments were sharper. Identity didn't shield poor thinking. Only truth did.

That spirit is missing in modern innovation processes. Often, ideas get filtered by status. A C-suite idea gets fast-tracked. An intern's idea? Buried. But what if you made it anonymous?

A digital payments company in Singapore launched an internal innovation drive but faced a recurring issue—most shortlisted ideas came from senior engineers or product leads. Junior staff rarely made it past the first round. So the company tried something new: the *"Nameless Sprint."* For two weeks, employees could submit innovation proposals using randomly assigned code names. No resumes. No department tags. Just pure ideas. A review panel of mixed seniority was assembled to judge based solely on clarity, creativity, and feasibility.

One standout idea—about integrating local hawker stalls into the digital payment ecosystem through QR-based micro-networks—was selected for funding. When the names were revealed, the panel was stunned: the idea came from a junior office admin who'd spent evenings helping her uncle run a food stall in Bukit Merah. Her lived experience gave her insight no market research ever could. She was immediately transferred to the innovation team and went on to co-lead the pilot program.

When you judge ideas on merit, you get innovation. When you judge on status, you get echo chambers. Hindu tradition teaches us that wisdom can come from anywhere—forest sages, warrior queens, street poets.

Modern Practice Tip:

Start an anonymous submission system for innovation pitches. Let panels review without identity bias. Reveal the creators only after shortlisting. This boosts fairness, freshness, and diversity of ideas.

10. Feedback Rituals

In every Hindu temple, the ritual is reciprocal. You offer something—flowers, prayers, effort. But you also receive something back: *prasad*. It's not just food. It's divine acknowledgment. That loop of giving and receiving is core to Hindu culture.

In business, we often treat feedback as a one-way street. Boss to report. Reviewers to employees. But innovation thrives when feedback is mutual—and when it's sacred.

At a design consultancy in Seoul, a team introduced a practice inspired by traditional Korean *jeong*—the deep bond formed through mutual care and respect. After each project sprint, they held a ritual called *"Cham-ui Banjak"* (meaning "Circle of Sincere Reflection"). The format was simple: each person shared one *gan-eunghada* (a moment of gratitude or appreciation) and one *baram* (a heartfelt wish for improvement). These weren't performance critiques. They were treated like offerings—spoken with humility, received with grace. Even the team leads participated equally, often starting by sharing where they felt they could have supported better.

In one session, a junior UX researcher shared how she wished the sprint lead had asked her opinion earlier in the process. Instead of reacting defensively, the lead bowed gently and said, "Thank you. I didn't realize I missed that." That moment reset the team's dynamic—and became a turning point in how leadership was practiced across the firm.

Over time, teams got sharper. Less passive aggression. More clarity. More experimentation. People felt heard—and seen. And when that happens, they try more. They risk more. That's how ideas are born.

Innovation isn't just about building. It's about *listening while building*. Prasad isn't just a gift—it's a sign your offering was received. Your feedback rituals should feel like that.

Modern Practice Tip:

End key meetings or projects with a “Blessing and Asking” round. Everyone shares one thing they appreciated and one thing they’d adjust. No debating. Just absorbing. Make it part of your innovation culture.

Conclusion

Lead Like a King, Listen Like a Sage

If there's one thing the Mahabharata, Ramayana, and Upanishads repeatedly teach us, it's this: great ideas rarely start at the top, but they die quickly if the top doesn't care. Leadership, in the Dharmic lens, isn't just about power—it's about the *protection and promotion of possibility*. Your role isn't just to direct strategy, but to *hold space* for discovery.

Every example in this chapter—from Janaka tilling the soil to Vishwakarma building celestial wonders—reminds us that leadership support is an active practice. It’s not just saying “yes” to a proposal. It’s sitting in circles, funding the foolish-sounding, mentoring the bold, backing the weird, and being willing to till your own fields once in a while.

In our AI-accelerated era, where data moves fast and decisions get automated, the most irreplaceable asset is human imagination. And that imagination only flowers in environments where people feel *backed*, not just managed.

So, if you're a leader, ask yourself: where in your organization can you be more like Krishna—calmly guiding, not commanding? Where can you be like Indra—trusting the builder even when you don't get the blueprint? Where can you show up like a *Guru*, not a boss?

Support is the fertilizer of innovation. Without it, even the best seeds will stay buried. With it? You get a forest.

Chapter - 6

Change-Based Agility

Flow Like Krishna, Shift Like Vishnu: Dharmic Wisdom for Fluid Innovation

Introduction: The Sacred Dance of Agility

There's a quiet moment before the arrow is released, when even Arjuna, the greatest archer of the Mahabharata, pauses—not to aim better, but to listen. To adjust. To align with the pulse of what's needed *now*. That pause, that moment of tuning in and responding fluidly—that's agility.

We often think agility is speed. Deadlines. Sprints. Frameworks. But real agility is not mechanical—it's emotional, intuitive, and contextual. It's not just being fast—it's knowing when to stop, when to pivot, when to drop the strategy and go with the flow. In the Hindu worldview, this isn't a new concept. It's ancient wisdom. From the adaptable rituals that evolved village by village, to the lunar calendars that gently guided when to build, rest, plant, or pray—life itself was agile. Our ancestors didn't resist change. They harmonized with it.

Now fast-forward to today—where AI is rewriting the rules every week, customer needs mutate monthly, and yesterday's five-year plan is today's meme. In this kind of world, the most successful organizations won't be the strongest or the smartest. They'll be the most agile.

In this chapter, we don't just study agility. We live it. Through the playful mischief of Krishna, the reinvention journeys of the Pandavas, the shape-shifting Dashavataras of Vishnu—we unpack how Indian cultural intelligence and Hindu mythic design offer a living manual for innovation in a fast-changing world.

If you've ever felt stuck in a corporate loop of "this is how it's always been done"—this chapter is your call to break that inertia. Because when you see how rhythm, ritual, rasa, and reinvention are already part of your DNA, you'll realize: you don't need to force agility.

You just need to remember it.

1. Apply Jugaad Thinking

Krishna was the OG innovator. From turning a stick into a flute to winning wars without lifting weapons, he exemplified the mindset of jugaad—doing a lot with little.

Imagine a scrappy student team in rural Maharashtra trying to solve crop loss issues during unexpected weather shifts. No incubator, no investor backing—just passion and pressure. With no laptops, they used a borrowed tablet from the local school. They pulled satellite data from free government APIs, cross-checked it with local WhatsApp farming groups, and converted the alerts into SMS-based weather guidance using a basic Twilio script one student had taught herself on YouTube. Their office? A repurposed storage shed near a temple. Their Wi-Fi? A shared mobile hotspot balanced on a cow shed roof for better signal. And yet, they managed to pilot the solution in three nearby villages. Farmers called it their "digital monsoon whisperer." That's not poverty—it's pure innovation through *jugaad.*

In Hindu society, resourcefulness isn't about being cheap—it's about being *aware* of what's available and being fearless enough to use it differently. Like when Krishna turned butter-thieving into a leadership lesson for his Gokul gang—mobilizing them for shared mischief, team bonding, and strategy under constraints.

In modern innovation? We waste too much. Too much budget. Too many tools. Too many "ideal" conditions.

Modern Practice Tip:

Run quarterly "Jugaad Sprints" where teams solve problems using only pre-existing internal resources. No new budget. No outside help. Watch creativity explode.

2. Adaptation Labs

Ayurveda never stopped evolving. Its formulas were tuned to seasons, body types, and patient feedback. Adaptability was built in—recipes updated with rain, climate, or even planetary positions.

Imagine if your product did the same.

Picture a learning platform in India originally designed to prep urban college students for government exams. It worked well—until COVID hit. Rural demand surged, but the platform wasn't built for patchy internet, local dialects, or the emotional stress learners were facing. Instead of patching the existing product with generic updates, the company launched an "Adaptation Lab"—a small, nimble team of designers, teachers, and two students from rural Bihar. They reimagined the platform: lessons were made offline-friendly, mental health check-ins were added, and the UI was translated into local scripts. Most importantly, the learning flow was redesigned for erratic schedules—like students who had to help in the fields during the day. Within three months, engagement in rural regions doubled. Not because they scaled, but because they *adapted*.

Adaptation is not just iteration. It's *relevance preservation.*

In India, that's how street-side Ayurveda thrived for centuries—always relevant, never frozen in time.

Modern Practice Tip:

Set up a mini Adaptation Lab inside your team. Pick an old product or process every month and refresh it for today's user. No launches—just learning.

3. Rapid Prototyping Rituals

Visit any Indian street food vendor. The guy who invented pani puri didn't do market research. He just mixed leftovers, saw people smiling, and iterated.

We need that energy in boardrooms. Fast, joyful experimentation.

Imagine a small Fintech startup trying to test a new interface for dyslexic learners. They didn't have time for a full design sprint, so the product manager grabbed a whiteboard, drew mock screens, and asked a local tuition teacher to narrate how a student might use each one. Then, they used colored index cards to simulate buttons and transitions. Within two hours, they had iterated three versions based on real-time reactions from two students nearby. One child said, "I like the blue box—it feels calming," and that offhand comment led to a full visual theme later validated by actual users. No Figma. No wireframes. Just cardboard, curiosity, and courage. That early version wasn't "minimal" for the sake of speed—it was minimal so they could truly listen.

In Hindu society, festivals are live prototypes—constantly updated rituals with hyperlocal flair. Even Diwali in Tamil Nadu and Punjab look different—same spirit, different execution.

Modern Practice Tip:

Institute "Friday MVP Rituals." Each team demos a raw prototype—no polish, just proof of value. Everyone cheers. Feedback flies. Agility soars.

4. Cross-Training Teams

Ancient temple builders weren't just masons. They were multi-skilled—often mathematicians, musicians, and sculptors. One carved pillars, calculated sun angles, and tuned bells. They understood the whole, not just the part.

That's what agility needs today—**multi-dimensional thinkers**.

Imagine a midsize logistics tech company struggling with coordination between its warehouse automation engineers and the operations team. As part of a cross-training initiative, a junior software engineer was sent to work two full weeks on the warehouse floor—scanning packages, rerouting deliveries, even dealing with customer complaints firsthand. At the same time, a shift supervisor from the warehouse shadowed the product team, sitting in on sprint planning and UX reviews. The result? The engineer redesigned the dashboard to show live package weights and delays—something no one thought to ask for, but which solved a constant floor-level pain point. The warehouse supervisor, meanwhile, became an unofficial UX advisor for the next rollout. Morale improved. So did performance. All because people swapped roles—and saw the system through new eyes.

The more perspectives you carry, the faster you adapt. In Indian gurukuls, education was interdisciplinary by default—philosophy, poetry, archery, logic—all integrated.

Modern Practice Tip:

Run a "skill switch week" quarterly. Rotate roles—designer to dev, PM to customer success. Make agility a felt experience, not a PDF.

5. Track Emotional Reaction, Not Just KPI

The *Natya Shastra* wasn't a dance manual. It was a framework for emotional transformation. It identified *rasas*—moods like wonder, love, and fury—as the true metrics of impact.

Yet, modern business still obsessively tracks KPIs without asking: *How did it make people feel?*

Imagine a mental wellness startup in Austin building a journaling app for teens. Their analytics dashboard was packed with metrics—retention, daily active users, session length. But something felt off. So the team introduced a new layer: an "emotion tracker" based on in-app emoji responses and voluntary mood reflections after journaling. One feature—a daily gratitude prompt—had the *lowest* completion rate but generated the *highest* number of heart and smile emojis, as well as dozens of spontaneous user comments like "this made my day" or "I needed this." It wasn't the most efficient feature—but it was the most beloved. The team doubled down on it, made it the app's daily centerpiece, and user love (and organic referrals) skyrocketed. That's when they realized: the feature didn't move metrics. It moved hearts.

In Hindu society, value wasn't just utility—it was emotional and spiritual connection.

Modern Practice Tip:

Add a "Rasa Meter" to product reviews. Rate features by emotional response—delight, confusion, curiosity—not just NPS or conversion.

6. Scenario Testing Like Krishna

Before the Mahabharata war, Krishna tried everything—diplomacy, escape, sacrifice. Every plan had a fallback. Every move, a counter.

Picture a consumer robotics startup developing a smart home assistant. They were prepping for a major launch, but instead of only creating a rosy roadmap, the COO insisted on running a "Krishna Table" exercise—three full days of scenario testing. They mapped out not just the ideal launch, but also a version where their supply chain collapsed due to a port strike, and another where a major privacy scandal broke in the industry the same week as their debut. In one session, an intern raised the question: "What if our AI misinterprets a child's voice command?"

That single what-if led them to build a fallback parental override protocol. Months later, a real delay hit—customs held a shipment in Singapore. Thanks to their scenario playbook, they rerouted hardware and launched on time. Investors called it luck. The team knew it was Krishna-level planning.

Agility Without Foresight Is Just Panic.

Modern Practice Tip: For every major product or strategy, write three versions: "Dream State," "Likely Reality," and "Disaster Pivot." Use these in all-hands meetings to build anticipatory muscles.

7. Use Lunar Cycles For Iteration

Hindu calendars run on *tithis*—lunar cycles that govern everything from agriculture to temple routines. They weren't just astrological—they were energetic blueprints.

Think of this: what if your team sprint aligned with natural ebb and flow? Imagine a 28-day cycle:

- Week 1: Ideate
- Week 2: Build
- Week 3: Test
- Week 4: Rest and Reflect

I've seen one UX team in Toronto, Canada use this model. Productivity shot up. Burnout went down. And their ideas had *soul*.

Modern Practice Tip:

Try a "Lunar Sprint Model" for 2 months. Let work flow with natural rise and fall—don't fight time, dance with it.

8. Rapid Pivot Rituals

The Pandavas were exiled for 13 years. Each year, they adapted—forest life, city disguise, war prep. Not once did they freeze in regret.

At a mid-sized tech company, the team had spent nearly a year developing a personalized study companion for high schoolers. It had all the bells and whistles—AI quizzes, gamified leaderboards, flashcard syncs. But after launch, student engagement flatlined. Instead of dragging the product forward out of ego or sunk cost, the founder instituted a company-wide ritual called "The Letting Go." Teams gathered quarterly in a town hall, where one underperforming feature or product was respectfully retired. They shared its original purpose, what it taught them, and wrote short "farewell letters" posted on the wall. One letter read: *"You were ambitious, but our users weren't ready. Thank you for the ride."* This emotional release made space for their next pivot—a lightweight group study tool that took off in just weeks.

It wasn't a shutdown. It was a conscious transition. A ritual of release. Like the Pandavas shedding roles to survive another phase, the team morphed without mourning.

Modern Practice Tip:

Run "Pivot Retrospectives." List what's outdated. Celebrate its contribution. Then pivot. Don't mourn; morph.

9. Mahabharata Roleplay For Decision-Making

Every character in the Mahabharata represents a different dharmic tension. Arjuna wrestles ethics. Bhishma holds loyalty. Krishna navigates strategy. Put them all in a room—and you get truth.

Imagine a Bengaluru-based healthtech company preparing to launch a controversial feature using predictive AI diagnostics. Instead of a typical boardroom debate, they hold a "Mahabharata Council." Each stakeholder takes on a dharmic archetype: the Head of Ethics becomes Arjuna, raising concerns about data consent and user autonomy. The CFO steps into Bhishma's shoes, defending long-standing revenue practices and legacy protocols. The CEO channels Krishna, urging everyone to think strategically—beyond compliance, toward societal impact. A young developer, embodying Draupadi, speaks for the vulnerable end-user—those most affected but least represented. The dialogue becomes layered, emotional, and revealing. By the end, they halt the rollout, redesign the feature with opt-in transparency, and—months later—it becomes their most trusted user tool.

Modern Practice Tip:

Try "Dharma Roleplay" in your next planning session. Assign mythic archetypes. Don't just brainstorm—storystorm.

10. Fluid Roles Like Dashavatara

Vishnu didn't show up as one fixed avatar. He became what the world needed—fish, boar, dwarf, warrior, sage. That's agility.

Today, specialists are great—but generalists who can morph are priceless. A marketer who can code. A CTO who sketches. A finance guy who can run HR for a quarter. I've seen it. These are your Dashavataras.

Picture a mid-sized SaaS company experimenting with what they call the "Dashavatara Rotation." Every quarter, team members are invited to embody a new role—not permanently, but as a sacred experiment. A UX designer becomes a customer success rep to feel the pulse of student feedback. A backend engineer takes over the company's Instagram for a week, learning storytelling. Even the CEO joins in, spending five days coding a bug fix with junior devs. This isn't chaos—it's intentional fluidity. The outcome? Empathy rises. Silo walls dissolve. And occasionally, someone uncovers a hidden superpower they never knew they had—like the accountant who became a beloved podcast host for the company's learning series. **Modern Practice Tip:** Let every team member explore one new skill domain per quarter. Make roles fluid. Innovation loves shape-shifters.

Conclusion

The beautiful paradox of agility is that it's not about becoming someone new every time. It's about remembering your essence, and expressing it **differently** as the world asks different questions.

Krishna didn't change who he was when he switched roles—from cowherd to kingmaker, from prankster to philosopher. He simply responded to context with grace, courage, and creativity. That's what modern innovators must do. Whether you're building AI workflows, navigating economic uncertainty, or launching new products—your tools will change, your roles will shift, but your purpose stays anchored.

Agility is not a project management style. It's **a worldview**. It's rooted in Hindu cosmology, where time is cyclical, roles are fluid, and every challenge is an invitation to evolve—not react. It teaches us that it's okay to change direction, to unlearn, to outgrow yesterday's successes. Because the true leader, the true creator, is not the one who sticks to the plan—but the one who can **rewrite the script mid-play** without losing the story.

So the next time a project stalls, a trend crashes, or a system breaks, don't panic. Pivot. Pause like Arjuna.

Reflect like Bhishma. Act like Krishna. And adapt like the Dashavatara.

Because in the end, agility isn't just how we survive disruption—it's how we **honor it**.

Chapter - 7

Dharma-Powered Design Thinking

From Sacred Systems to Smart Solutions:
Ancient India Engineered for the Future

Introduction: Why Technology Needs a Soul

Let's step back for a moment and ask something simple—but dangerous:

Are we building tech that makes life better… or just faster?

Look around. We've automated everything. We've built systems that write for us, schedule for us, talk for us, even *think* for us. But in the middle of this hyper-efficiency, people are burning out. Screens get smarter while humans get lonelier. Notifications get louder while our inner clarity grows faint. Somewhere along the line, the spirit got left behind.

But here's the wild part: this is not a *new* problem.

Thousands of years ago, our ancestors in India were asking the same thing—not in digital labs, but in the temples, forests, and towns of Bharat. They asked, "How do we build in harmony with the world? How do we design tools that don't just function—but *uplift*?" Their answers weren't slideshows or product specs. They were *embodied principles*—engraved into stepwells, encoded in mantras, carved into musical stone.

Every instrument had an intention. Every tool had a soul.

Temples were not just places of worship—they were energy systems engineered with cosmic alignment. A plough wasn't just for farming—it was blessed before use. A chisel was handled with reverence. Innovation didn't just mean "new." It meant "*true* to dharma."

And that's the difference.

In today's world of rapid iteration and generative breakthroughs, what we desperately need is **sacred intention**. We don't just need to ship fast. We need to ship *wisely*. We don't just need to build things that work. We need to build things that *heal, harmonize, and elevate*.

This chapter is your call to remember that.

The ten principles that follow aren't rules. They're reflections—meant to provoke, challenge, and stretch how you think about leverage, design, and innovation. These ideas are not about going "backward" into tradition—they're about moving *forward* with roots. Because a tree that forgets its roots can grow tall, yes—but not for long.

So if you're tired of shallow sprints, if you feel like tech is losing its meaning, if you want to build something that feels *true*—not just trendy—then walk with me.

We're going to learn from the ancients—not to imitate them, but to be inspired by their **deep, slow, purposeful genius**.

1. Internal Demo Days

Picture this: a master sculptor in 10th-century Tamil Nadu, standing before the king and temple patrons, hammer in hand. Before carving the deities into the stone pillars, he demonstrates a technique on a test block. The king nods. The patrons give feedback. Adjustments are made. Only then does the actual carving begin. That was the ancient version of internal demo day—and it was genius.

Now fast-forward to a modern office. Teams slave over a product in stealth for 8 months. They finally launch it... and nobody wants it. Why? Because nobody gave feedback along the way. There was no cross-functional rhythm. Everyone worked in silos, assuming alignment.

Internal demo days change that. They create a culture where showing incomplete work is *not a weakness*, but a strength. Just like artisans trusted their community to co-shape the output, demo days build trust, catch issues early, and bring in perspectives you never thought mattered.

What if your firm introduced demo days and engineers began understanding why sales always pushed for that "tiny tweak." Designers would start to build with backend constraints in mind. Suddenly, innovation wouldn't be a linear pipeline—but a living dance.

Modern Practice Tip:

Block off one Friday every month. Teams share their half-baked ideas, sketches, or early prototypes. No pressure. Just presence. What gets seen early gets built better.

2. Learn from Ancient Technologies (Vimanas, Stepwells)

We talk a lot about "smart cities" today, but let me take you to Dholavira—an Indus Valley city from over 4,000 years ago. It had a full water conservation system, integrated sewage, and natural ventilation—all without wires, sensors, or electricity. It was smart before "smart" existed.

And then there's the story of Maya Danava—the legendary asura architect in Hindu texts who built flying vimanas, palaces in the sky, and even automated illusions for gods. His mastery wasn't just technical—it was cosmic. Every structure he built respected geometry, elemental balance, and purpose.

So what can we learn from this? Ancient India didn't treat technology as separate from life—it embedded it *within* life. It wasn't about consumption, but about coherence. That's the difference.

Today, in our rush to optimize, we forget elegance. We over-engineer. But when I helped a sustainable architecture firm study stepwells and temple layouts, we came up with low-energy cooling systems that outperformed high-tech ACs in cost and durability. Less flash, more function.

Modern Practice Tip:

Start a monthly "Ancient Tech Inspiration Jam." Pick one Indian structure—stepwell, temple, Vimana lore—and ask: what can we learn from this for our modern product, office, or platform?

3. Spiritual Engineering Labs

Let me tell you about the Chidambaram temple. From a distance, it looks like a standard Dravidian temple. But step inside, and the architecture starts playing with your senses. The sanctum is aligned to the magnetic axis of the

Earth. The flooring geometry reflects the periodic table. The main deity is... nothing. Space itself. *Nataraja dances in emptiness.*

That's not architecture. That's spiritual engineering.

Now think about your tech product. Your app. Your dashboard. Does it generate calm? Focus? Joy? Or does it stress people out with 18 notifications, dark UX patterns, and dopamine loops?

The best tech is invisible. It fades into the background and lifts the human spirit. When I worked with a wellness app team, we redesigned their interface inspired by temple layouts—minimal UI, breathing space, focused entry paths. Churn rate dropped by 30%. Coincidence? I don't think so.

Sacred space matters. And in the digital world, every screen *is* a space. You're either building a temple or a circus.

Modern Practice Tip:

Introduce "Digital Vastu" reviews. Audit your product flow not just for clicks, but for emotional resonance. Where's the calm? Where's the noise?

4. Partner with Rural Innovators

You want frugal innovation? Go to the villages.

There's a guy in Gujarat who built a windmill out of junkyard parts to power his irrigation pump. Another in Maharashtra turned a discarded bicycle into a washing machine. They weren't doing this for TED Talks. They were doing it because they had to. No VC funding. Just sharp observation and zero ego.

Picture this: a consumer electronics company in Delhi hosts a rural innovation showcase as part of their annual R&D retreat. Among the invitees is a farmer from Odisha who demonstrates a grain-drying contraption made entirely from repurposed scooter parts and clay tiles. At first, the urban engineers chuckle—until he reveals it cuts post-harvest loss by 30% during unpredictable rains, using zero electricity. One lead engineer pulls him aside afterward and asks, "Could we adapt this airflow system for off-grid cooling in our smart homes division?" That one conversation sparks a prototype—merging rural ingenuity with urban ambition.

Rural innovation thrives under constraint. It prioritizes need over novelty. These inventors solve problems we didn't even think to notice—and they do it with elegance.

We don't need to give rural India our tech. We need to bring their wisdom *into* our tech.

Modern Practice Tip:

Set up a "Jugaad Exchange" once a quarter. Invite rural problem-solvers to share their ideas with your product team. Build something *with* them—not for them.

5. Tech for Dharma

Every year during Navratri, my grandmother would clean her sewing machine, place flowers on it, and light a diya. As a kid, I thought it was cute. Later, I realized: she was doing Ayudha Puja—the worship of tools.

Not for superstition, but to remind herself: "Use this tool for good. Never for harm."

That hits different when you're building algorithms today.

Tech today is so powerful it can make or break lives. An AI model used unethically can deny people jobs, insurance, or loans. A recommender engine can polarize elections. Every tool we build carries karma.

I worked with a digital media startup once. They had a high-engagement feature that was... frankly, addictive and toxic. We shut it down and replaced it with a reflection prompt feature. Usage dropped slightly—but user trust rose. Investors balked at first. But long-term? It paid off.

This is tech for *dharma*. Not just efficiency. But alignment with what uplifts.

Modern Practice Tip:

Create a "Dharma Audit" process. Every quarter, ask: is our tech harming someone unintentionally? Are we creating addiction, exclusion, or fear? If yes—course-correct.

6. Human-Centric Design via Ayurveda

Ayurveda isn't just a medical system. It's a *philosophy of personalization.* It says: no two people are alike. Everything—your routine, your medicine, your food—should adapt to your inner rhythm, season, and context.

Now apply that to UX.

Imagine a wellness-tech startup designing an app for caregivers of elderly patients across India. Instead of defaulting to standard reminder notifications, they created an Ayurvedic-inspired interface where users could choose their "daily dosha state": grounded (Kapha), active (Pitta), or reflective (Vata). Based on the selection, the app adjusted tone, color schemes, and even the pacing of suggested tasks. One week, a user in Kerala picked "Vata" during monsoon season and received slower, calmer prompts and more journaling cues—reducing stress and boosting usage consistency. Feedback rolled in: "It feels like the app knows me."

Design that adjusts to the user—not the other way around—is the future. Just like Ayurveda doesn't treat the disease but the *person*, our systems must serve the user as a dynamic, whole being.

Modern Practice Tip:

Redesign your UX flows to include user-led rhythm settings. Morning vs evening modes. Focus vs creative states. Build adaptive tech, not rigid funnels.

7. Train AI on Multilingual Indian Sources

Most AI models are biased—not because of intention, but because of *input*. They're trained mostly on English and Western data. But India? India has 22 major languages, hundreds of dialects, and millennia of oral tradition.

In the Panchatantra, the same moral story appears in Sanskrit, Tamil, and Awadhi—with different phrasing, humor, and rhythm. That's cultural intelligence.

If your AI doesn’t know Bhojpuri metaphors or Tamil sarcasm, it’s not "smart." It’s just elite.

Picture a conversational AI startup in Hyderabad trying to build a mental health chatbot for rural Indian youth. Their first prototype, trained mostly on English and Hindi corpora, misunderstood key expressions. A Telugu-speaking teen said, “Naku gundelo gubbillu vuntunnayi” (literally: “I feel like pigeons are fluttering in my chest”)—a poetic idiom for anxiety. The bot flagged it as joy. Realizing the gap, the team partnered with local universities to ingest folklore, folk songs, and regional proverbs in Telugu, Odiya, and Maithili. The result? The bot didn’t just translate—it began to **feel** local. Engagement shot up. One user said, “It speaks like my grandmother.”

Diversity in training data doesn’t just improve accuracy—it *expands intelligence.*

Modern Practice Tip:

Build a multilingual data sourcing team. Go beyond translations—train AI on native narratives, idioms, and regional patterns. Your global relevance depends on it.

8. Non-Tech Mentorship From Craftsmen

One of the most transformational experiences I ever had was shadowing a potter in Kumbakonam. He didn’t talk much. He didn’t need to. His hands spoke. Every movement had rhythm, economy, and grace. Watching him, I realized: tech teams need less jargon, more *flow*.

Imagine a startup in Jaipur that paired its product team with local blue pottery artisans for a week-long immersion. One of the engineers, initially skeptical, found himself mesmerized by how the artisan aligned each curve of a hand-painted bowl without using a single measuring tool. “I don’t calculate,” the craftsman said. “I calibrate with breath.” That sentence stuck. Back at the office, the engineer began rethinking his UI transitions—not in terms of milliseconds, but in terms of visual breathing room. Button placements became more rhythmic. Animations slowed just enough to feel intentional. User drop-off declined.

You don’t need a new framework. You need a new *feeling* for form.

Modern Practice Tip:

Launch a "Craft to Code" mentorship week. Pair product leads with master artisans. Observe. Absorb. Let material intelligence shape digital thinking.

9. Reverse Innovation from India

Everyone thinks innovation flows from Silicon Valley to the world. But in healthcare, mobility, and sustainability, India often leads.

Take Aravind Eye Hospital: they perform thousands of surgeries per week, at under $30 each, with clinical outcomes better than in the U.S. Or the Jaipur Foot: a $45 prosthetic that gives dignity back to millions.

These aren't just low-cost hacks. They're full-stack design ecosystems—optimized for scale, access, and human dignity.

Picture this – a global medtech company based in Boston wanted to expand to low-resource regions in Southeast Asia. Their flagship surgical scheduling software had cutting-edge features—calendar sync, AI optimization, patient flow analytics. But once they piloted it in rural Odisha, it failed miserably. Power outages, low digital literacy, and spotty Wi-Fi made it unusable. Instead of abandoning the effort, they studied how Aravind Eye Hospital managed thousands of surgeries using colored folders, marker boards, and a "runner" system. Inspired, the company developed a hybrid model: a low-code tablet app with offline syncing and tactile physical cards for scheduling in real time. The result? It's now their fastest-growing product in three continents—not despite its simplicity, but because of it.

Simplicity is not a limitation. It's a lens.

Modern Practice Tip:

Do a "Reverse Innovation Hackathon." Start with the assumption: "We have $10 and no electricity." Now solve a problem. That's where the magic lives.

10. "10% Budget" Innovation Days

Monks in the Himalayas spend weeks making intricate mandalas from colored sand—only to wipe them away in seconds. It's not nihilism. It's training. You don't build for permanence. You build for *presence.*

Imagine a large U.S. software company announcing a "10% Budget Innovation Day" once a quarter. No fancy tools, no slide decks, no budget approvals. Just markers, reused office paper, and analog clocks to keep time. At first, the senior engineers smirked. But by noon, teams were sketching wildly creative product ideas—like a healthcare app interface inspired by board games and a chatbot that mimicked the tone of local diner waitresses. One team even built a prototype demo using Post-it notes, string, and a flip phone. The ideas weren't just clever—they had heart. It wasn't about constraints for constraint's sake; it was about unblocking buried creativity. Everyone agreed: they hadn't felt that *present* in a brainstorm for years.

Constraints birth elegance. When you have everything, you invent nothing. When you have nothing—you create *from source.*

Modern Practice Tip:

Host a "No Tech Innovation Day." No devices. No slides. Just whiteboards, recycled paper, and imagination. You'll meet parts of your brain you forgot existed.

Conclusion Code with Consciousness

If you've made it this far, I want you to pause. Not because the ideas are over, but because your own reflections are about to begin.

Because let's face it—this chapter wasn't just about tools. It was about *you*. About how you, as a designer, leader, coder, or creator, choose to walk the path of innovation.

Not every line of code changes the world. But every line of code *shapes* something—a behavior, a thought, a habit, a moment in someone's life.

And that's power.

The question is: are you using that power with awareness?

When ancient sthapatis built temples, they didn't rush. They aligned every stone with the stars. When potters made clay lamps, they whispered mantras into the wheel's spin. When village inventors built water carts out of scrap, they didn't see it as "jugaad"—they saw it as seva. This wasn't poetic idealism. This was technical wisdom grounded in consciousness.

We need that again.

In a time when AI can do more than most humans ever imagined, what will make your product *matter* isn't speed or scale. It's *soul*. Your tech doesn't need to be perfect—it needs to be purposeful. It needs to serve something beyond profit. It needs to leave behind *karma* that future generations won't have to clean up.

The real innovators of the next decade won't be the fastest. They'll be the *wisest.*

So, build like your code is a prayer. Design like your product will enter a temple. Write algorithms like your grandparents will use them. Bring in dharma—not as nostalgia, but as navigation.

Because this is our moment—not just to disrupt, but to *heal*. Not just to accelerate, but to *align.*

Technology is your hammer. But what you build with it? That's your legacy.

Chapter - 8

Strategic Vision

See Beyond the Quarter - Building Tomorrow with Ancient Eyes

Introduction: The Sacred Compass of Innovation

In every age, visionaries have shaped the future not by merely looking ahead—but by learning to look within and behind. Strategic vision isn't about trend forecasting or having a bullet-point strategy deck. It's about developing a *sacred compass*—an inner and outer alignment of values, time cycles, stories, ethics, and possibilities. The Hindu dharmic worldview gives us tools to do just that.

In the modern corporate world, we often equate strategy with speed and metrics. But in the Indian tradition, strategy is soulful. It is layered, like the *Arthashastra*. It is cyclical, like the *Yugas*. It is value-rooted, like *dharma*. And it is often told through stories—*itihasa*—which are not just history, but "so it was," a poetic truth meant to awaken strategic clarity.

This chapter invites you to widen your lens. To think like Vishnu, evolving across ages. To plan like Krishna, moving through grey zones of diplomacy. To reflect like Ashoka, hosting debates rather than declaring decisions. And to track your ideas like rishis, with reverence for lineage.

Strategic vision is not about predicting the future—it's about preparing to *create* it. With meaning. With ethics. With intergenerational courage. These next ten ideas (Points 71–80) are not just business tools—they're cultural templates to help you innovate not just faster, but wiser.

So pause. Breathe. Imagine you're sitting under a banyan tree, sipping chai with Chanakya, Krishna, and Janaka. What would they advise? Probably this: strategy is not just what you do. It's who you become while doing it.

1. Write Roadmaps Like Epics

In the tech world, a roadmap is often a sterile chart with dates, features, and vague milestones. But what if your roadmap was more like *The Ramayana*? What if your product journey read like an epic—where your customer was the hero, your obstacles were demons, your beta testers were Hanuman, and your team was the vanara sena helping to bridge the gaps?

Take Rama's story. His mission wasn't just to rescue Sita. It was about upholding dharma in the face of chaos, traveling through forests, meeting sages, winning allies, losing and finding hope. His journey wasn't linear, and neither is innovation. There were pivots. There was grief. There was redemption. And like any great roadmap, it was driven by a purpose bigger than himself.

Now imagine you're building an AI-driven healthcare app. Instead of just listing "Phase 1: Patient onboarding" or "Phase 2: Chatbot Q&A," you narrate it like an epic. "In Act 1, our hero—the patient—faces confusion in diagnosis. In Act 2, they meet their digital ally. By Act 3, they reclaim their health confidence through empowered insights."

Why does this work? Because stories make strategy stick. The human brain remembers stories 22x better than data points. When your dev team knows they're not just writing code but helping a character cross a metaphorical ocean to reach healing, they're fired up. And when your investors hear the roadmap as a mission, they're drawn into your gravity.

Even Indian classical dances like Kathak or Bharatanatyam, which depict tales from the *Ramayana*, show that innovation isn't about jumping from A to Z. It's the choreography in between. It's the nuance, the grace, the interpretation. Similarly, in business, your roadmap isn't just what you'll build—it's how you'll help someone transform.

Strategic vision isn't just about what's next. It's about what matters. Ramayana reminds us that destiny is earned, not guaranteed. So, craft your journey with meaning, not just motion.

Modern Practice Tip:

Don't just make a roadmap—write a strategic story arc. Name each phase like a chapter in an epic: "Crossing the Forest," "The Bridge to Lanka," "Return with the Crown." This makes vision magnetic and internal alignment powerful.

2. Dashavatara Strategy Map

There's this brilliant evolutionary metaphor hiding in plain sight in Hinduism—Vishnu's ten avatars, or *Dashavatara*. It's like a startup's product lifecycle told through divine archetypes.

Vishnu starts as a fish (*Matsya*)—agile, essential, and meant for survival. Then comes *Kurma* (turtle), slow but foundational—like your infrastructure layer. Then *Varaha* (boar), lifting the Earth from chaos—think early disruption. Next, *Narasimha* (man-lion), raw protection—think regulatory battles. Each avatar reflects society's evolutionary needs, culminating in *Kalki*, the warrior on a white horse—cosmic alignment, peak innovation.

What does this teach us? Strategy isn't static. It must evolve with your user's consciousness, your market's need, and society's maturity. You can't push a *Kalki*-level feature to a *Matsya*-level user base. The mismatch kills.

For example, a fintech startup may begin by offering basic savings (*Matsya*) for financial inclusion. Then, over time, it adds budgeting tools (*Kurma*), insurance offerings (*Varaha*), credit assessment engines (*Narasimha*), and eventually AI-based wealth coaching (*Kalki*). It's a strategic unfolding—not a launch-day dump.

Hindu civilization thrived because it understood this rhythm of release. Temples evolved from caves to multi-sensory complexes. Scriptures evolved from oral chants to epic poems to sutras. Every age, every yuga, brought new avatars—of Vishnu and of vision.

Think of your product like this. What version are you offering now? What level is your market ready for? What's the next avatar you'll evolve into?

Modern Practice Tip:

Design a "Dashavatara map" for your product. For each user maturity level, map a new feature or offering. Ask: What does our user need at this evolutionary step? Don't overbuild for an unevolved market.

3. Lineage Mapping of Ideas

In India, knowledge didn't just happen—it was transmitted, curated, and honored. From sage to student, through *parampara* (lineage), ideas carried not just content but context.

In the *Bhagavad Gita*, Krishna reminds Arjuna that this wisdom was first passed to the Sun God, then to Manu, and down the royal sages. This isn't ego—it's innovation ancestry. Knowing your lineage helps you innovate consciously.

Let's bring this to the boardroom. Imagine you're building a new sustainability feature. If you trace the idea's roots, you realize it came from an intern's early pitch, which was inspired by a customer complaint, which in turn echoed a government policy shift. Suddenly, this feature isn't just a JIRA ticket—it's a legacy node.

In modern teams, we often erase idea ancestry. Products morph and mutate without context. But tracing lineages allows us to preserve intent, avoid past mistakes, and show reverence for collective effort. It's like Vedic chanting—each intonation passed precisely through centuries. Accuracy mattered. So does acknowledgment.

In AI, lineage mapping becomes vital. Models inherit biases from data, which came from authors, who lived in societies. By tracing this chain, we ensure ethical and intentional evolution.

Let's not lose our lineages. Let's document our brainstorms, name our internal contributors, honor the small voices that became big features. Culture builds through storytelling, not Jira tickets.

Modern Practice Tip:

Create an "Idea Family Tree" for major features. Include sources, inspirations, blockers, and heroes. Review it quarterly. It builds gratitude, clarity, and compounding wisdom.

4. Dharma-Aligned Visioning

The Mahabharata is full of dharma dilemmas. Bhishma follows one kind. Karna follows another. Yudhishthira never lies—except when dharma demands it. That's the thing: *Dharma isn't a rule. It's a compass.* And your company needs one too.

When startups chase growth without dharma, they win users but lose trust. When leaders pivot without a moral center, they breed confusion. But when your strategy aligns with core human values—like dignity, fairness, community—you don't just make products. You make meaning.

Consider a conceptual example: imagine a U.S.-based fintech startup facing pressure to increase user acquisition numbers before Series A funding. One advisor suggests using urgency-based pop-ups with countdown timers—classic dark pattern psychology. But instead, the founder proposes a radical experiment: no manipulative language, just clear opt-ins and transparent educational walkthroughs about loan risks. Investors grumble. Growth is slower at first. But six months later, customer retention doubles. Users aren't just clicking—they're trusting. The company earns a reputation as the "ethical lender," leading to organic referrals and a surprise partnership with a public credit union. Their dharma wasn't growth at any cost—it was building financial dignity for underserved users.

In Hinduism, dharma differs by role. A warrior's dharma isn't the same as a sage's. Similarly, your sales team's dharma may be persuasion. Your product team's dharma may be empathy. But the overarching vision must unify.

Dharma visioning means asking not just, "What can we do?" but "What *should* we do?" In a world of AI, this matters more than ever. When algorithms decide credit scores or jail terms, dharma isn't optional—it's oxygen.

Modern Practice Tip:

Build a "Dharma Canvas" for your strategic plans. Ask: Who does this help? Who could this harm? What deeper value does this serve? Make ethics part of roadmap reviews.

5. Impact KPIs Beyond Profit

Ever visited a temple in Tamil Nadu or Odisha? You'd see students reciting slokas, elders feeding pilgrims, women weaving garlands, and sick people getting herbal treatments—all under one roof. That's design thinking. The temple wasn't just spiritual—it was social infrastructure.

Today's companies chase "EBITDA" and "CAC," but ignore "healing per user" or "community uplift per click." That's a narrow lens. Hindu philosophy reminds us that true success serves many layers—body, mind, spirit, society.

There's a startup in India building sanitation infrastructure. Their dashboard tracks not just usage but dignity—how many women felt safer? How many girls stayed in school? That's real innovation. Because when you measure impact, you inspire it.

Strategic vision must widen its metrics. Are we hiring from underserved areas? Are our tools making users feel seen? Are our AI models inclusive in voice and vernacular?

Profit is fuel—not the destination. Hinduism teaches us *artha* (wealth) is one of four life goals, but not the only one. There's *dharma* (right action), *kama* (joy), and *moksha* (liberation). Business needs to evolve beyond shareholder supremacy.

Modern Practice Tip:

Add a second KPI tier to your dashboard—track access, dignity, joy, or sustainability. Review these in quarterly all-hands alongside financials.

6. Long-Term Debates Like Ashoka's Council

After the bloody war of Kalinga, Emperor Ashoka didn't just repent—he redesigned governance. He convened councils of Buddhists, Jains, and Brahmins to debate national ethics. Imagine that—a quarterly board meeting with monks.

In your company, when was the last time strategy included a philosopher or a social worker? Or even a contrarian developer? We build echo chambers that sound efficient but slowly kill innovation.

Long-term visioning needs diversity—not just of skin tone, but of thought, ethics, and inquiry. When you put a climate scientist, a poet, and an AI engineer in the same room to talk about product vision, magic happens.

Debate isn't about friction. It's about sharpening. The Upanishads are structured as dialogues. *Neti Neti* ("Not this, not that") is the process of peeling layers. Why should corporate visioning be less curious?

Don't fear disagreement. Institutionalize it. Ashoka's brilliance wasn't in having the answers—but in building a house where all questions could be asked.

Modern Practice Tip:

Host annual "Council of Curiosity" events—invite artists, ethicists, and domain misfits to debate the future of your company. Publish learnings.

7. Council of Sages Model

Imagine a startup founder who thinks of themselves as King Janaka—not because of ego, but because Janaka always sought counsel from sages like Yajnavalkya. Before launching anything big, he asked: "What does this mean for my people?"

In your company, before you ship, who do you ask? Your dev team? Legal? Good. But where's the culture voice? The customer advocate? The ethics whisperer?

Strategic vision must include a circle of sages. Not just MBAs, but real-world seers—designers, sociologists, spiritual thinkers, community leaders. The Arthashastra says kings should consult people from all four varnas before major decisions. It wasn't hierarchy—it was holistic thinking.

When Apple removed the headphone jack, they likely had a product council—but maybe not a culture council. Hence the backlash. When Patagonia designs, it consults environmentalists before marketers. That's sage-thinking.

Sages don't just warn. They illuminate. In your team, appoint guardians of dharma, not just deliverables.

Modern Practice Tip:

Set up a Strategic Sage Circle—cross-functional, diverse in domain and perspective. Before major launches, hold reflective sessions asking: "What are we missing?"

8. Quarterly Era Reflection

Time in Hinduism isn't linear—it's cyclical. There's *Satya Yuga*, when truth prevails. Then *Treta*, *Dvapara*, and finally *Kali Yuga*—when everything gets murky. But here's the kicker: no yuga lasts forever.

Your company, too, lives in eras. What worked last year may be obsolete today. The product-market fit of yesterday is the product-market misfit of tomorrow. Yet most strategies assume a straight line.

Quarterly reflection helps you ask: "What yuga are we in now?" Are we in a build era or a prune era? Are we still in "growth at all costs," or are we in "depth over reach"?

Netflix began as DVD shipping. Then streaming. Now gaming. Each yuga needed different values, talent, and metrics. Their survival depended on reflection.

In the Mahabharata, even Krishna withdraws when his era ends. That's vision. Knowing when to pivot, not from panic—but from deep timing.

Modern Practice Tip:

Every quarter, hold an "Era Review." Ask: What assumptions no longer serve? What cycle are we closing? What season are we entering?

9. Intergenerational Thinking

In many Indian households, planting a Peepal tree wasn't about aesthetics—it was a legacy act. The tree wouldn't give shade for 30 years. Yet people planted them anyway. That's vision.

Modern startups chase viral growth, MVPs, and “fail fast” loops. But who’s designing for 2070? Who’s building for grandchildren?

A temple like Brihadeeswara took generations to build. Its architects knew they wouldn’t live to see it completed. Yet they carved every stone with devotion.

You too can design like this. Build knowledge bases that will outlive your team. Design UIs with aging users in mind. Make ethics so embedded that future hires feel them in the onboarding doc.

When you think in decades, you stop chasing dopamine and start building dharma.

Modern Practice Tip:

Include a “Next Generation Lens” in product design. Ask: Will this be usable, respectful, and sustainable for someone 30 years from now?

10. Use Arthashastra Planning Logic

Chanakya didn’t believe in single-track plans. His *Arthashastra* integrated diplomacy, warfare, ethics, espionage, economics, and education. It was a startup manual disguised as statecraft.

When launching a new initiative, don't just think “go-to-market.” Think: What alliances are needed? What counter-narratives will emerge? What ethical blind spots might explode later?

A Fortunte 500 CEO divided their product launch into 5 tracks: Product Design, Policy Alignment, Public Narrative, Partner Play, and Ethical Review. That's Arthashastra in motion.

Chanakya was ruthless but not reckless. He taught that strategy was not just about speed—it was about layers. Multiple parallel bets. Contingency stacks. Reputation shields.

You don't need to read Sanskrit. Just read the room—and design multiple levers.

Modern Practice Tip:

Adopt "5-Lane Strategic Planning": for every initiative, plan across Product, Policy, People, Partners, and Philosophy. This builds robust, resilient innovation.

Conclusion

As we close this chapter on strategic vision, one truth becomes evident: in a world racing toward innovation, it's the ones who *remember* that truly lead. Remember what? The past. The soul. The end user. The ripple effects across generations.

Each of the ten principles in this chapter offers a dimension of vision that is both eternal and timely. From writing roadmaps as epics to evolving your strategy like the avatars of Vishnu… from building councils of sages to measuring impact beyond profit… we are reminded that strategy is never just a spreadsheet. It's a story. A prayer. A responsibility.

The Hindu tradition doesn't separate logic from spirit, or metrics from meaning. And neither should we. Because the future we're building with AI, data, and tech will be barren unless rooted in values that outlast the quarterly cycle. When we think like sages and act like innovators, we make decisions that endure.

So what will your company be remembered for? Features? Or foresight? Speed? Or soul?

Let your strategy not just disrupt—but *heal*. Let your innovation not just scale—but *serve*. And let your roadmap not just chart the next sprint—but *ignite the next generation*.

That is strategic vision, the dharmic way.

Chapter - 9

Circular Resourcefulness

The Dharma of Doing More with Less

Introduction: Reverence, Constraint, And Cycle-Based Thinking Drive True Innovation

We often think innovation is born in labs, on whiteboards, in billion-dollar R&D centers. But I'd argue some of the greatest innovation I've ever witnessed came from a chai vendor in Jaipur who used the same dented pot for three generations, or from a tribal schoolteacher in Odisha who built teaching aids out of bottle caps and mud.

Resourcefulness isn't just a workaround. It's a worldview.

In the Hindu and broader Indian cultural imagination, every object, person, and process is part of a living web. A leaf is not waste—it's a plate. Ash isn't garbage—it's soap. A failed prototype isn't junk—it's a seed. What seems disposable in a modern context was, and still is, sacred in many parts of India. This instinct to reuse, repurpose, and reflect deeply on usage isn't poverty thinking—it's wisdom thinking. And in the modern business world, it might just be one of our most underutilized tools for innovation.

Think about it: AI is transforming how we build, code, learn, and create. But AI also consumes staggering resources—data, energy, compute. In this era of abundance, the companies that will truly lead aren't just the ones who have the most, but the ones who **use what they have with reverence**. As innovators, our job isn't just to create—it's to conserve, to reinterpret, and to give new life to the old.

This chapter is about that sacred practice: seeing value where others see waste, turning limitations into sparks, and reclaiming the lost art of frugality as a virtue—not a restriction. Rooted in Hindu traditions, each of the next ten lessons reveals a deeper truth: real innovation doesn't come from having everything. It comes from **knowing the value of anything.**

1. Run Frugal Design Reviews

Imagine standing in the heart of Mohenjo-daro, an urban marvel from over 4,000 years ago. The Harappans didn't have steel or modern engineering degrees. But what they did have was staggering clarity and intention. Homes were arranged in grids, shared walls reduced material use, every brick was standardized for interchangeability, and public water systems recycled greywater to irrigate food gardens. It was design not for opulence, but for harmony and interdependence.

Their genius was not in extravagant building but in subtle decisions—modularity, placement, and shared access. They optimized not for display but for collective dignity and sustainability. This is the kind of frugality that breeds real innovation—where limits provoke elegance, not mediocrity.

In modern businesses, we often get lost in the glamour of "what's possible" and forget to ask, "what's necessary?" When budgets inflate, designs become bloated. When timelines are comfortable, creative urgency dissipates. But if we evaluate our product blueprints, feature ideas, and campaign proposals the way the Harappans planned their cities—with precision, restraint, and collective efficiency—we can birth designs that not only perform better but age better.

Frugality, then, isn't about stinginess—it's a virtue. One that says, "I respect the time, space, and resources available to me enough to use them with integrity."

Modern Practice Tip:

Integrate a "frugality score" into every design sprint and product roadmap—evaluate not just what the idea does, but how much it demands. Reward those who achieve beauty through elegant minimalism.

2. Celebrate Repurposing

There's a beautiful moment in many Indian homes where a faded silk sari—no longer suitable for wear—is laid out, ironed flat, and turned into a *kantha* quilt. Each thread that once swayed in weddings or prayers is now stitched into something warm, new, and equally meaningful. This act of transformation isn't just practical—it's poetic. It honors the past while gifting it a renewed future.

In the Hindu view of time and life, nothing is ever truly finished—it simply changes *rupa* (form). Old manuscripts become bedding for calves. Cracked temple bells are melted into statues. Coconut shells, once emptied, become lamps or kitchen tools. This circularity is not accidental—it is dharmic. It reflects an understanding that all things are part of a larger flow, and the wise mind rides that flow instead of constantly starting from zero.

Modern corporations, in contrast, tend to dismiss what's "old." Old codebases? Trash them. Previous campaign drafts? Archive them. Past experiments? Forgotten. But there's buried gold in all of it. That botched MVP? Maybe the architecture is reusable. That unused brand slogan? Perhaps it belongs to the new product line. Repurposing, when celebrated, makes our systems regenerative rather than extractive.

And the act itself builds team confidence. When a designer sees their failed idea transformed by a peer into something extraordinary, it reminds them: nothing is wasted—not even your failures.

Modern Practice Tip:

Initiate quarterly "Repurpose Labs"—where teams are challenged to build something entirely new using only pre-existing assets. Offer rewards for the most elegant reinvention.

3. Zero-Waste Internal Challenges

When I visited a tribal kitchen in Odisha, I noticed something remarkable. The ash from the wood-fire stove was collected in a small earthen pot. Later that evening, it was mixed with lemon peel and used to scrub utensils. Not only was there no waste—there was no concept of waste. Every by product had a second life, a future role.

This mindset, deeply ingrained in rural India, arises not just from poverty, but from reverence. It's an awareness that all matter is energy, and wasting it is an ethical failing. In traditional Indian households, food is prepared with exactness so that none is thrown away. Even banana peels might be turned into chutney or used in gardening.

What if our organizations adopted this reverence? Not just in physical resources, but in human energy and digital assets? Think about how much output in a given month adds no value—dead meetings, bloated reports, features no one uses, dashboards no one reads. It's all waste. Not because it's toxic, but because it's unconscious. Because we didn't pause to ask: what could this be instead?

Sustainability isn't just for PR reports—it's a creative challenge. The more constraints you embrace, the more ingenuity you demand from your teams. Waste, then, becomes a signal—of laziness, of haste, of unrefined design.

Modern Practice Tip:

Institute a "Zero-Waste Week" once a quarter. Teams must operate without disposables, repeat content, or low-impact meetings. Debrief what was gained—and what was surprisingly unnecessary.

4. Old-to-New Creative Days

Every spring, as Holi approaches, the Indian subcontinent comes alive with bursts of color. What most don't realize is that in its earliest forms, Holi wasn't about commercial powders or industrial dyes—it was a celebration of the *leftover*. Fallen flowers from winter were dried and crushed into color. Spices and herbs past their culinary prime became skin-safe pigments. In short, Holi turned residue into revelry.

That spirit is powerful when applied to innovation. In today's fast-paced business environments, teams are often under pressure to constantly deliver "new." New features. New campaigns. New frameworks. But sometimes the most novel ideas aren't born from fresh inputs—they emerge when we revisit what's been abandoned.

There's something creatively humbling about taking an old prototype, a discarded idea, or a feature that never made it to launch, and giving it a new destiny. It forces teams to see with different eyes. It cultivates the ability to spot potential where others saw waste. Like an artist working only with charcoal and ash, the constraints don't hinder creativity—they become the source of it.

And it sends a quiet message to your team: nothing they create is worthless. Even in "failure," something of value remains. If that mindset is nurtured, people won't fear experimentation. They'll trust that their efforts will always find a place—now or later.

Modern Practice Tip:

Host an "Old-to-New Day" each quarter. Gather failed mockups, outdated research, old strategy decks—and ask teams to create something beautiful from them. The rule? Use only what already exists.

5. Kubera's Constraint Challenge

Kubera is often depicted as rotund, jeweled, and regal—the treasurer of the gods, guardian of wealth. But his mythos holds a deeper lesson: despite his abundance, Kubera was never reckless. His wealth came with boundaries, ritual discipline, and cosmic responsibility. In fact, when he failed to honor balance, his fortunes were said to become cursed—teaching that prosperity without mindfulness is decay disguised as growth.

This is a hard truth for modern organizations. When resources are abundant, it's tempting to overbuild, overhire, overdesign. But over time, those bloated systems collapse under their own weight. What if, instead, we trained teams to create with the spirit of Kubera—not in scarcity, but in sacred restraint?

Imagine asking your product team, "Design this solution as if you had only 10% of your current resources." What you'll see is a shift in thinking. Suddenly, assumptions get questioned. Core value becomes clearer. Creativity is unleashed—not in spite of the limits, but because of them.

The challenge isn't to think small—it's to think smart. Like Kubera, wealth (or in our case, budget and time) should be treated not as license, but as a test: can you multiply it? Can you extract maximum value from minimal input?

Modern Practice Tip:

Host an annual "Kubera Challenge" where every department must solve a pressing business issue using only a fraction of their usual resources. Share stories of the most inventive outcomes company-wide.

6. Sustainability Metrics Per Feature

In many Indian homes, the act of lighting a lamp is sacred. But beyond the symbolism lies subtle design wisdom: the lamp doesn't just illuminate—it purifies the air, marks a shift in energy, and brings warmth. Every object in traditional Indian life had multiple functions—often physical, emotional, and spiritual. The cow, for instance, provided milk, dung for fuel, labor for fields, and was also a religious symbol. Multipurpose utility was the norm, not the exception.

Fast forward to our current software economy, and this design philosophy feels more relevant than ever. Most product teams measure success in clicks, time-on-site, and engagement loops. But rarely do they ask: what's the moral footprint of this feature? What kind of human behavior is it incentivizing?

We must reintroduce the idea of ethical sustainability into our feature design. Not just "does it work?" but "does it uplift?" Does it simplify life or complicate it? Does it create harmony or dependency? This is a deeper, subtler form of resourcefulness—where the outcome is not just a deliverable, but a contribution to wellbeing.

Sustainable innovation is not about restraint—it's about intention. When features are designed with deeper awareness, they last longer, serve broader audiences, and gain trust.

Modern Practice Tip:

Build a "Sustainability Scorecard" for features. Measure not just usability but long-term ethical impact, cognitive load, and user flourishing.

7. Internal Economy (Trade & Barter)

In the ancient cities of India, before coins were widespread, people traded skills and goods through a complex dance of trust. A blacksmith might offer tools in exchange for cloth. A sculptor might carve a temple statue in return for food and lodging. These weren't temporary arrangements—they were entire ecosystems of mutual dependency and cultural wealth.

Now look at modern companies. Everyone operates in silos. Need help from another team? You raise a ticket, or worse, wait in line. But what if your internal structure worked like a living marketplace, where people could trade time, skills, and tools like ancient bazaar dwellers?

A designer might offer five hours of Figma time in return for support from the data team. The operations team could trade documentation assistance for legal support. Suddenly, people aren't just exchanging labor—they're building empathy, cross-functional visibility, and culture.

This economy doesn't need tokens or trackers. It needs a mindset that sees abundance in collaboration—that knows we're all sitting on skills someone else desperately needs.

Modern Practice Tip:

Start an "Internal Barter Board." Let teams list what they can offer and what they need—encouraging organic, respectful, peer-to-peer exchange across silos.

8. Study Temple Economies

Temples in India weren't just spiritual centers—they were economic dynamos. The Jagannath Temple in Puri employed hundreds of cooks who served thousands of meals daily, funded entirely by community donations. The Meenakshi Temple in Madurai owned land, ran educational programs, and served as a central planning unit for civic life. They built systems not to extract value, but to recirculate it.

Their model was simple yet profound: take in wealth through devotion and redistribute it as social infrastructure. Even in their rituals, the intent was clear—abundance was meaningful only when shared.

Modern innovation hubs can learn a lot from this. Too often, labs become isolated centers that produce IP for the top-line or vanity metrics for the boardroom. But what if your innovation lab operated like a temple economy? Serving the community, nurturing internal talent, and reinvesting lessons into open ecosystems?

Imagine a lab where part of every successful product went toward mentoring young developers, or where unused features were donated to NGOs as open-source tools. That's not generosity—it's intelligent regeneration.

Modern Practice Tip:

Structure your innovation unit to "give back" 10% of time, profit, or learning into internal education, community partnerships, or emerging markets.

9. Community Resource Hackathons

Attend a community-run festival in India and you'll witness a miracle: massive infrastructure with no central planner. Streets light up with handmade decorations, temporary kitchens feed thousands, and entire processions emerge—all powered by volunteer spirit, local craftsmanship, and shared intent.

This is distributed innovation at its finest. No outside consultants. No imported tools. Just trust, hustle, and local resourcefulness.

That same spirit can be infused into corporate innovation through community-powered hackathons. But not the kind with fancy budgets and keynote speakers. I mean grassroots challenges where teams use only existing tools, local data, and peer knowledge. No plugins. No outsourcing. Just ingenuity.

These kinds of hackathons break down dependency. They remind teams that innovation is a mindset, not a tech stack. And most importantly, they build a culture of collective ownership.

Modern Practice Tip:

Host "Barefoot Hackathons"—challenges where only existing internal tools, free resources, and team-level collaboration are allowed. No new purchases, no expert hires—only collective wisdom.

10. Teach Through Daan & Seva

There's a profound line in the Bhagavad Gita: *"Whatever you give in charity, do it as an offering to Me."* In Hindu dharma, giving—*daan*—and service—*seva*—are not just good deeds. They are means of personal and societal evolution. A king builds a stepwell not for fame, but to serve generations. A teacher shares knowledge not for payment, but for continuity of truth.

This dharma of giving can radically transform how innovation is practiced. What if mentorship wasn't a bonus activity—but a built-in part of leadership? What if companies routinely released their retired IP to educational institutions or grassroots startups?

When you teach someone your method, when you offer your codebase to an under-resourced team, when you give away your design frameworks—it might look like you're losing competitive edge. But in truth, you're doing three things: clarifying your own thinking, inspiring new use-cases, and shaping the next generation of builders.

That's not just generous—it's brilliant strategy.

Modern Practice Tip:

Start a "Seva Sprint" every six months—teams must dedicate time to build something valuable for a cause, NGO, or younger startup, using your internal expertise.

Conclusion

We've spent this chapter exploring what it means to be truly resourceful—not just in the startup sense of "bootstrap hustle," but in a deeper, more intentional sense that's encoded into thousands of years of Hindu life and practice.

From Harappan cities to temple economies, from the joyful reuse of Holi's colors to the quiet generosity of seva, India teaches us that resourcefulness is not an emergency strategy—it's a mindset. It's how civilizations last for millennia. It's how knowledge survives without being patented. It's how innovation is democratized, decentralized, and distributed—without ever needing a logo or a funder.

As a modern leader—whether you're in tech, design, strategy, or sustainability—the lesson is simple: Your resources don't define your innovation. Your **relationship** with those resources does.

So look again. That "waste" material on your product roadmap might be your next breakthrough. That intern with no title might carry the insight no one else sees. That budget cut you dreaded might be the best thing that ever happened to your process.

Resourcefulness is not the art of survival—it's the art of transcendence. It teaches us to see the sacred in the small. To honor every byte, every breath, every barrier as an invitation to stretch further. And most of all, to innovate not with excess, but with essence.

So next time your team groans about what they don't have—ask them this: **What can we do with what we already do?**

Because when we create from dharma—not just data—we don't just ship better products.

We Build Better Worlds.

Chapter - 10

Embracing Experimentation

Experimentation as a Path to Insight, Growth, and Innovation

Introduction: The Sacred Art of Trying

There's a quiet courage in trying something new.

Not because it's guaranteed to succeed, but because you're willing to risk being wrong, misunderstood, or even laughed at. In our modern business world—especially in the age of AI, automation, and predictive analytics—there's a growing illusion that everything must be precise, proven, and optimized before it's ever attempted. But innovation doesn't bloom under such pressure. It blooms in play. In detours. In sacred trial.

The ancients of Hindu society understood this well. They created environments where experimentation wasn't just allowed—it was ritualized. Think of the Ayurvedic healer testing herbs with patience, or the temple dancer exploring movement through years of subtle improvisation. Think of artisans who made ten iterations of a diya lamp not to maximize profit, but to find the one shape that made the flame dance longer. These weren't random acts. They were mindful, intuitive, and often spiritual.

Experimentation in the Hindu worldview is *tapasya*—a practice. A discipline. And a joy. It's not about failing fast or pivoting constantly. It's about becoming sensitive enough to notice what the world is trying to tell you. Whether through street theatre, feedback rituals, metaphorical prompts, or co-creating with nature and community—these practices can still teach us to make room for the unexpected.

As we walk through these final ten principles of innovation—from mythological prototyping to public curiosity modeling—ask yourself: Do I give myself the permission to experiment? Do I give others that freedom? Do we, as teams, actually play? Because the more sacred we make experimentation, the more radical our innovations can become.

1. Monthly Freeform Innovation Days

Hindu Reference: In the concept of a *Kalpa*—a cosmic day of Brahma—there is time for divine play (*lila*), not just order. Similarly, many sages had *anavasara* days—time off from ritual to reflect, roam, or just observe the sky.

Imagine a mid-sized UX consultancy in California. The head of design proposes something she calls “Lila Fridays,” inspired by the idea of sacred play. No deliverables. No agendas. Instead, team members can sketch wild interface concepts, explore bizarre user journey maps, or even repaint parts of the office wall. One junior designer spends the day building a tactile feedback prototype using cardboard, string, and a smartphone’s vibration motor—just to see if haptic rhythm could influence user calmness. It had no immediate business purpose. But that prototype ended up inspiring a pitch to a wellness app client that became their biggest win that year.

Modern companies talk a lot about ‘innovation time’ but it’s often boxed into slides and frameworks. The real magic? It happens when there’s no agenda. Like the *lila* of Krishna—joyous, free play—it's about the spirit of flow.

And let's be honest—our brains need oxygen. When you tell your team, "You have a day to do anything…no judgment, no review," you unlock parts of their soul that are usually compressed under tasks and tickets.

Picture a conceptual scenario at a biotech startup in Singapore. On their first "Zero Outcome Wednesday," a backend developer builds a meditation timer that syncs with lunar phases—just for fun. A marketer scribbles out a comic strip explaining genomics to children. A QA engineer explores how mudras (hand gestures) could be used as non-touch inputs in wearable health devices. Nobody asked them to do it. But two months later, during a pitch to a Southeast Asian hospital chain, these experiments become the centerpiece. The client says, "You think differently." That comment sealed the deal.

What I realized was this: productivity is not about doing more. It's about creating space where meaningful things can emerge.

Modern Practice Tip:

Schedule one day each month where employees are free to build, explore, or play—no approvals, no KPIs. Treat it like a festival, not a formality.

2. Test Like an Ayurvedic Healer

In Ayurveda, *vaidya* healers didn't just apply herbs blindly. They tested on fruits, animals, and eventually themselves. Each stage taught something nuanced—texture, smell, reaction, patience.

Story: Innovation isn't about rushing—it's about reverence. The ancient *vaidya* understood that nature speaks slowly. A new herb couldn't just be added to a medicine. First, you'd observe its color. Then boil it. Then rub it on a fruit. Then apply it to a goat. Only after stages of understanding would the healer consider trying it on a person.

This sounds slow—but it's profoundly intelligent.

In today's world, we're obsessed with A/B testing. But how many of us really *observe* the results beyond a number on a dashboard?

A conceptual example comes to mind: imagine a mid-stage wellness tech startup in Seoul, South Korea inspired by Ayurvedic methodology. Instead of launching their new AI sleep coach to the entire user base, they structured their testing in layered phases—first with just five internal team members, then fifty long-time users, and only then a wider release. But here's the twist: after each phase, they didn't rely solely on click-through rates or retention curves. They hosted "listening salons"—intimate video calls where users shared how the tool made them feel. One participant said, "It feels too robotic… like it's judging me for not sleeping." That offhand comment changed everything. They rewrote the AI's tone to be more nurturing, inspired by the voice of a grandmother from Korean folktales. That update became their standout feature—and the app's five-star reviews skyrocketed. All because they tested like a vaidya: in layers, with sensitivity, and with soul.

Guess what? One of their failed features—a self-check symptom tracker—was reimagined after seeing user hesitation in a meso rollout. They added humor. A talking *vaidya* cartoon. The new version went viral. But it wouldn't have happened if they rushed to scale.

Testing is not about speed. It's about *sensing*.

Modern Practice Tip: Use a three-phase test approach—small, medium, large. After each phase, hold structured qualitative feedback circles, not just dashboards.

3. Co-Create with Traditional Makers

Indian artisans—like Kanchipuram weavers or Kondapalli toy-makers—have passed down techniques for centuries. Each innovation came from touch, rhythm, and knowing materials like kin.

One summer, I visited a temple town in Tamil Nadu where I saw a weaver working on a 12-yard Kanjivaram saree. It wasn't just silk. It was a story. It was pattern logic. He said, "My father taught me to listen to the tension of the thread. If it hums wrong, it's not ready."

What struck me was how he *felt* innovation, not just designed it.

In the West, we talk about "user research." But indigenous artisans are themselves users of their own tools and products. Their feedback loop is built into their fingers.

Imagine a conceptual case: a climate-conscious architecture startup in Pune wanted to tackle the rising heat problem in low-income housing. Instead of pulling only from engineering textbooks or Western green design manuals, they initiated a "Listening Residency" with local potters and tile-makers in a village outside Kolhapur. For two weeks, their design team sat under mud-tiled roofs, touched clay as it cured, and asked one question: “How do you feel temperature shift?” An elder potter shared that the way she layered clay shards with jaggery and husk helped her food stores stay cool—even in May. That single insight inspired a prototype of layered “breathable bricks” for modular housing, blending old wisdom with modern forms. The results? Cooler interiors, lower costs, and a product now being trialed in slum redevelopment projects.

When we bring traditional makers into the design room, we don’t just get new products—we reconnect to sensory knowledge lost in abstraction.

Modern Practice Tip:

Run co-creation labs with traditional craftspeople—masons, tailors, cooks. Let them influence design based on feel, not just spec.

4. Visible Experiment Logs

Ancient Indian texts—*granthas*—painstakingly recorded treatments, temple measurements, rituals, and seasonal changes. These weren’t just notes—they were evolving knowledge bases.

Story: In the Charaka Samhita, every herb trial was recorded—what time of day it was picked, which season it thrived in, and what symptoms it addressed. It was part science, part art. The core idea? Make knowledge communal.

Now imagine this in a modern workplace.

Picture this: a mid-sized design-tech company in Hyderabad set up something they called the "Yatra Journal." It wasn't just a log—it was a living experiment diary. Every time someone tried a new prototype, pitch deck format, or onboarding script, they had to write a short entry. But here's the twist: they were encouraged to log emotional notes too—what they *expected*, how they *felt*, what surprised them. One entry read: "Tried removing all bullet points from the investor deck. Felt nervous. Investor smiled more than usual." Another: "Added temple bell sound to app launch. Calmed me down. Client said nothing—unclear impact."

Within three months, new hires said the journal was their favorite onboarding tool. Instead of just being handed SOPs, they inherited a consciousness—why certain choices were made, where experiments had failed, and what unspoken truths the team was learning. It became not just documentation, but a cultural archive.

Logging your experiments isn't about bureaucracy. It's about building a *shared brain*.

Modern Practice Tip:

Create a company-wide experiment log or wiki. Make it visible. Add thoughts, feelings, not just data.

5. Honor Failure Like Epic Plot Turns

Ram's exile. Karna's betrayal. Draupadi's humiliation. These were not the end. They were turning points that unlocked the next act. Failure was necessary for transcendence.

We often hide our failures. Or worse, we sanitize them.

But think of the Mahabharata. Every hero fails. Bhishma lies on a bed of arrows. Arjuna breaks down in paralysis. Krishna loses loved ones. These weren't bugs in the story—they were the point.

Now imagine this: a mid-sized edtech startup in Pune initiated a quarterly ritual called "The Yuddha Tales." The premise was simple—each team had to choose one major failure from the past three months and reframe it as an episode from an epic. They'd present it like a performance—costumes optional, metaphors encouraged. One team turned a failed product integration into a courtroom drama, complete with a mock trial of the "culprit" feature. Another retold a missed partnership deal as a mythic romance gone wrong, where "Business Development" played the over-eager suitor and "Legal" was the reluctant in-law.

At first, it felt silly. But something profound happened. Laughter opened up vulnerability. People admitted things they usually hid—assumptions, shortcuts, ego traps. Junior employees saw senior leaders own their stumbles. No one lost face. Instead, they gained perspective.

A new hire said it best in their onboarding feedback: "This is the first place where failure is treated like a rite of passage, not a report card." Over time, this ritual began shaping decisions. Teams paused more before launches, sanity-checked assumptions, and wrote postmortems that actually got read. All because failure wasn't buried—it was honored, like a plot twist in a shared story.

Failure isn't the opposite of success. It's the soil of it.

Modern Practice Tip:

Host storytelling retrospectives of failures. Make it fun, human, and dramatic. Let teams narrate the "epic plot twist" moments.

6. Food Labs as Innovation Exercises

Indian kitchens are living R&D labs. Every home chef—especially grandmothers—experiments daily with ingredients, proportions, and improvisation based on availability and intuition.

If you've ever watched an Indian grandmother cook, you've seen what real iteration looks like. No measuring cups. No rigid instructions. Just a bit more hing here, a dash of tamarind there. "Taste and see," they'll say, nudging you forward.

To explore this idea, imagine a product team at a mid-size design agency in Chennai. The creative director introduces something called "Kitchen Kombat Thursdays." Each week, cross-functional teams are given a mystery basket of traditional ingredients—say, raw mango, coconut, and ragi—and challenged not only to cook something edible but also to extract an innovation metaphor from the process.

One week, a team accidentally burned their ragi dosa. Instead of tossing it, they ground it into a crispy crumble and turned it into a topping. Their insight? "What breaks can also become garnish." They tied this to a product failure they had earlier in the quarter—realizing they could repackage failed features as learning modules for junior designers. The cooking experiment led to a fresh internal training product. The kitchen, in this case, wasn't a detour from innovation. It was a catalyst for it.

Cooking, like innovation, is deeply sensory. You must taste as you go. Feel the heat. Pivot fast.

Modern Practice Tip:

Host culinary innovation days. Mix food-making with team ideation. Creativity rises when hands move and the senses awaken.

7. Street Theatre for Testing Ideas

Hindu Reference: In Ram Leela and Yakshagana, mythological stories are enacted live in villages. The audience gives instant feedback—gasps, laughs, even corrections mid-performance.

When I was a kid, I watched a Ram Leela in Varanasi where the actor playing Ravana forgot a line. An old uncle in the front row shouted, "He didn't say that in Lanka!" Everyone laughed—but the play continued. Real-time feedback, zero ego.

That night stuck with me.

Now imagine a young startup in Ahmedabad, Gujarat developing a new eco-friendly packaging concept. Instead of hosting a closed focus group, they decided to set up a mock street stall during the city's Sunday flea market. Dressed in costume like mythological characters—one person as Hanuman handing out samples, another as Sita explaining the story behind the biodegradable wrap—they turned the test into a mini street play.

Crowds stopped. Kids pointed. Some aunties commented, "Why is Sita selling soap?" Others remarked, "If Hanuman believes in it, maybe I should too." But here's what mattered: people talked, joked, critiqued. A grandmother even suggested replacing the wrap's floral print with turmeric-yellow motifs, saying, "It'll feel more pure." That spontaneous insight made it into their final brand palette.

In just two hours of public performance, the team gathered more actionable feedback—color, placement, tone, emotional response—than they had in weeks of internal brainstorms. It wasn't polished research. But it was real.

Modern Practice Tip:

Prototype new ideas in live, customer-facing environments. Farmers markets, pop-ups, live-streams—embrace real-time feedback.

8. Model Curiosity Publicly

Rishis weren't all-knowing—they were question-askers. The Upanishads are full of dialogues where sages admit doubt and engage in inquiry. Curiosity wasn't weakness—it was sacred.

There's this beautiful story where the sage Yajnavalkya is challenged by Gargi, a woman philosopher, with deep metaphysical questions. He doesn't scoff. He listens. He engages. He even says, "If I do not know, I will say so."

That's power.

In modern offices, especially at the top, curiosity is often seen as a junior trait. But true leadership models *questioning*, not just declaring.

A VP at a product company I know began starting every meeting with a "Question I don't know the answer to." Her team followed suit. Within months, innovation skyrocketed—because curiosity was culturally validated. When a leader says "I don't know—let's find out," it's like spiritual oxygen.

Picture this: A mid-sized edtech company in Southeast Asia launches a new initiative called *"Ask Like a Sage."* At the beginning of each leadership meeting, the CEO chooses one Upanishadic-style question to ponder—something like, "What part of our platform might be making students feel unseen?" or "Where are we assuming clarity when confusion might exist?" These aren't rhetorical. Everyone is encouraged to reflect, even if they don't have immediate answers.

Soon, department heads join in. A head of product admits, "I don't fully understand how a 12-year-old in a remote village experiences our onboarding flow." That vulnerability becomes a project. A cross-functional team runs field visits, builds empathy maps, and rewires the interface. Not because someone demanded innovation—but because someone dared to wonder aloud.

Modern Practice Tip:

Have leaders model curiosity publicly. Start meetings with real questions. Reward not just answers, but good, deep questions.

9. Prototype Using Mythological Scenarios

Hindu myths are full of imaginative what-ifs. "If Krishna had a chariot in today's world…" or "What if Hanuman ran a logistics company?" The absurdity unlocks creativity.

Imagine a design sprint at a product studio in Chennai called *Mythos Lab*. Instead of traditional brainstorming, the facilitator says, "Today's challenge: You are part of Rama's exile team. You have no internet, but must coordinate 3 million vanaras across forests. What do you build?" Another prompt reads: "You are Yudhishthira, stuck with moral paralysis. Design a tool that helps weigh dharmic options in real time."

One group imagines a rugged offline mesh communication tool, "MonkeyMesh," using ultra-low-frequency signals—intended for disaster zones. Another team drafts a mental health platform called *"Dharma*

Compass," where users input complex emotional choices and receive guidance styled like a guru's wisdom. They base its design logic on Gita verses, but present it through gentle, visual storytelling.

It was all fictional. But the freedom to step out of modern constraints let teams explore strange, sacred, and strategic patterns. One participant said, "We weren't just designing features—we were designing from feeling, ethics, and imagination."

It sounds wild, but these metaphors bypass mental blocks. They open up logic, empathy, emotion, ethics—all at once.

Myths are imagination machines. They are ancient prototypes of human behavior. Using them can spark modern innovation that's both meaningful and fun.

Modern Practice Tip:

Use mythological or cultural scenarios as prompts in ideation sessions. Encourage the surreal—it's a shortcut to deep creativity.

10. Feedback as Sacred Ritual

After temple visits, devotees often sit quietly in reflection. What shifted inside them? What did they feel? This sacred closure is as important as the act of worship itself.

In many temples, after offering prayers, people sit facing the deity—not to ask more, but to reflect. "What did I feel?" "What truth came to me?" It's feedback, but from within.

A conceptual example: Imagine a product studio called *Anvesha* based in Pune. After each design sprint, they hold what they call a "mandala closure." The team gathers around a rangoli-style chalk circle on the floor. No laptops. No dashboards. Just a single diya in the center. Each member speaks one sentence beginning with: *"What this sprint taught me about myself was..."* No crosstalk, no replies—just presence. One developer admitted he'd been rushing without listening. A junior designer said she realized she feared suggesting bold ideas. There were tears once. And laughter too.

They found that in this space, feedback wasn't performative. It was transformative. It wasn't about velocity—it was about voice. One engineer later said, "I write cleaner code because I feel cleaner inside." That's the power of sacred feedback—it shifts not just product metrics, but personal meaning.

Feedback isn't a metric—it's a ritual. It's how we return from the experiment and ask: "What did it show us about ourselves?"

Modern Practice Tip:

Create a ritualized feedback process. Not just surveys—but sacred, structured reflection. Make closure meaningful.

Conclusion

If there's one thing we should take away from this chapter—and this book—it's this: Innovation isn't a one-time event. It's a cycle. A loop. A sacred rhythm of trying, reflecting, adjusting, and trying again.

In the rush to scale, to disrupt, to monetize, we sometimes forget the human side of experimentation. We forget that behind every great invention was someone who wondered aloud. Who sketched a silly idea. Who tried something that didn't work, and still showed up the next day. That courage? It's not modern. It's ancient. It's woven into the DNA of Hindu culture—from the grand cosmic experiments of Brahma to the humble culinary innovations of every Indian grandmother.

So what can we do today, in the age of ChatGPT and quantum computing? We can remember what our ancestors knew: that real innovation requires presence. Ritual. Reflection. Curiosity. And the willingness to walk paths where no results are guaranteed.

Let's not reduce experimentation to A/B testing or corporate jargon. Let's elevate it to what it truly is—a sacred space for wonder, for learning, and for becoming more alive to the possibilities around us.

Try. Reflect. Share. Repeat. That is the rhythm of dharmic innovation.

And as you finish this chapter, maybe take a small experiment of your own. Not because it'll work, but because you'll grow.

Chapter - 11

Culturally Rooted Innovation

Designing with Roots, Rituals, and Regional Identity

Introduction: The Rooted Future

There's something quietly revolutionary about looking backward to move forward.

In our globalized world of unicorns, agile sprints, and algorithmic decisions, we often chase innovation as if it's a disembodied force—floating in some sterile cloud server, measured only in KPIs and VC decks. But what if true innovation isn't just in the "next big thing"? What if it also lives in the long-forgotten, the locally lived, and the culturally sacred?

You see, in India, innovation has always had soil under its nails. It comes wrapped in ritual, seasoned with mythology, and shaped by the pulse of place. From the way a potter learns by feel, to how elders narrate epic wisdom without reading a line, culture is not an obstacle to innovation—it is its original blueprint.

This chapter is an invitation. An invitation to see design not just as a process but as a prayer—an alignment of people, purpose, and place. It is a gentle provocation to stop trying to be "global-first" and instead become glocally wise. To pause and ask: *Are we designing from somewhere? Or just for everywhere?*

In the age of AI, where we risk flattening out identity in pursuit of scale, culture-centric innovation becomes an act of creative resistance. It roots us. It reminds us that our future must still feel like home.

Because no matter how advanced our technology becomes, people will always want to feel seen, heard, and honored—in the language they speak, through the symbols they trust, and within the stories they live.

1. Design Around Ritual Rhythms

In India, it's common to see businesses delay their grand openings until a pundit (aka priest) confirms the "shubh muhurta." Farmers wait for specific moon phases to sow seeds. Even buying a car or starting a job comes after consulting an astrologer. Now, you might roll your eyes if you're from a hyper-rationalist world, but here's the thing—these aren't just superstitions. They're community-wide alignment tools. Ritual rhythms create collective anticipation, emotional readiness, and even spiritual synchronization.

When Flipkart ran sales during Diwali or when Tata releases budget cars during Gudi Padwa, they weren't just marketing—they were aligning with a deeper cultural pulse. Think of it like surfing—you don't create the wave, you ride it at the right moment. The innovation lies in sensing the wave before it crests.

The ancient Hindu calendar, the Panchang, isn't just a timekeeper—it's a behavior map. It tells you when to celebrate, when to mourn, when to reflect, and when to act. That's powerful behavioral insight for any innovator.

Modern Practice Tip:

Use local calendars to time your product launches, feature rollouts, or customer nudges. Sync with festivals, agricultural cycles, or school calendars. Let rhythm—not just logic—guide your timing strategy.

2. Respect Local Knowledge as Sacred

There's a village in Gujarat where homes are built with cow dung, lime, and earth. They're naturally cool in summer, warm in winter, and resistant to pests. Any modern architect would pay thousands for that level of sustainable design. Yet, many dismiss it as backward.

In the Hindu worldview, even what seems "dirty" can be divine. Gobar isn't just waste—it's fuel, antiseptic, insulator, and even symbolic of purity when smeared at the threshold of a home. The Vedas teach us that nothing in the cosmos is without value—every object holds potential depending on how you look at it.

So, here's a thought: maybe local village practices aren't primitive—they're simply unexplored IP.

Modern Practice Tip:

Audit local customs for untapped innovation. Talk to rural artisans, farmers, or homemakers. Document their processes. Then ask—what if this was a patented solution? Reframe your R&D to look inward before importing from Silicon Valley.

3. Use Myth as an Interface Metaphor

Every product has a user journey. But most journeys are dry—steps, checkboxes, confirmations. What if it could feel like a Mahabharata arc?

In the Bhagavad Gita, Arjuna begins confused and paralyzed. With Krishna as guide, he confronts doubt, gains clarity, and eventually takes empowered action. This is literally the emotional arc of any user trying a new product or system.

Startups could map onboarding around this. Let users explore their confusion ("Arjuna's Moment"), meet guidance ("Krishna's Tips"), test knowledge ("Kurukshetra Challenge"), and finally achieve mastery.

Metaphors shape memory. When you say "we're in the churning of the ocean stage"—any Indian immediately knows you're talking about chaos, emergence, and the birth of amrit. That's the power of shared story structures.

Modern Practice Tip:

Infuse your product flow or change management process with cultural myth metaphors. People resonate deeper with narratives than with manuals. Use them to shape emotional flow.

4. Map Regional Archetypes, Not Just Personas

In the West, personas are flat: "Ramesh is a 32-year-old digital native who likes fitness." That tells you nothing about his lived reality. But in Indian cultural design, archetypes carry whole worlds.

Take the "banjara" (nomadic trader). He values movement, adapts fast, and respects stories more than titles. Or the "gurukul student"—obedient, ritual-driven, and learning-oriented. Designing for these archetypes helps you speak to their motivations, not just their demographics.

Even today, an Indian mother may respond better to a "pujari's daughter" persona than a "tier-2 female homemaker aged 34." One connects emotionally; the other is data.

Modern Practice Tip:

Work with anthropologists or sociologists to map cultural archetypes in your target market. Use these to build more authentic products, campaigns, or service flows. Speak identity, not just behavior.

5. Design for Sacred Spaces, Not Just Functional Ones

The Indian home always has a corner for the divine. Even in the most tech-enabled families, a small puja shelf sits quietly with incense and light. It's not about religion—it's about rhythm, intention, and reverence.

In offices, we've lost that. Everything is speed, screens, and noise. But what if your innovation lab had a silence corner? Or your app had a "pause and reflect" mode before big decisions?

Indian temples are masterclasses in experience design. From gongs that recalibrate your hearing to fragrant flowers, soft lighting, and rhythmic chants—they design an altered state of mind. They prepare you for inner work.

Modern Practice Tip:

Incorporate sacred pauses into your designs. Create zones of quiet in office spaces or digital products. Add rituals of opening and closing. Respect the human need for depth—not just output.

6. Leverage Cultural Symbols for Trust

The swastika in India is auspicious (unrelated to the hateful Nazi Hakenkreuz). A kalash at the door signals purity. A diya means welcome. These symbols do more than decorate—they transmit values non-verbally.

When a fintech app uses lotus motifs and Sanskrit-inspired typography, it tells the user: "We understand your roots." Trust builds. Not because of features—but because of familiarity.

This isn't just design—it's dharma-driven branding. In a culture where visual semiotics carry generational memory, design decisions aren't aesthetic—they're ethical.

Modern Practice Tip:

Audit your UI, packaging, or architecture for local cultural cues. Add trusted symbols where appropriate. Let visual familiarity build emotional security and open adoption pathways.

7. Prototype with Community, Not Just For It

Have you ever seen a temple being built in a village? It's not outsourced to contractors. Everyone pitches in.

Women carry stones, elders chant blessings, kids mix clay. It's messy, but beautiful.

This is shramdaan—voluntary labor for shared sacred purpose. It's also the original design sprint.

Modern teams often bring in "user voices" at the end—for validation. But traditional Indian society brought them in at the beginning—for co-creation.

Want real innovation buy-in? Let the people help shape it.

Modern Practice Tip:

Turn your prototyping into a collective ritual. Bring users, elders, artisans, and skeptics into the room early. Use paper, clay, and conversation. Make it sacred. Make it shared.

8. Design for Oral, Not Just Literate Cultures

The Vedas weren't written down for thousands of years. They were sung. Perfectly memorized and passed down. Sound was the storage medium.

Even today, vast parts of rural and low-income India prefer oral information. They trust a video more than a PDF. They'd rather hear from a local influencer than read a policy document.

In innovation, we overindex on reading. Terms & conditions. Onboarding text. Product manuals. But real inclusion needs oral design.

Modern Practice Tip:

Use voice assistants, regional dialect videos, and rhythmic onboarding (think jingles or chants). Test your product with someone who can't read—but loves to listen. That's real accessibility.

Conclusion

What we call "culture" isn't just colour and festivals—it's infrastructure. Invisible, emotional infrastructure. It shapes trust, emotion, aspiration, rhythm, and behavior. And when you build your innovation strategy on that infrastructure, you're not just being "inclusive." You're being *intelligent*.

In a hyper-connected world, sameness is easy to scale. But meaning? Meaning requires intimacy. It requires that we show up to a village meeting, sit on the floor, listen to elders, observe a seasonal ritual, learn a lullaby, hear a myth. That's how you build products—and futures—that belong.

This chapter explored how India's spiritual and societal fabric already contains timeless innovation strategies. From syncing with planetary cycles to co-designing with the community, from designing for oral-first cultures to leveraging symbolic trust—these aren't exotic traditions. They're **unfair advantages** waiting to be unlocked.

And maybe that's the deepest truth: that the most advanced innovations will not come from fleeing our roots, but from composting them into fertile ground for the future.

So as you walk into your next design sprint, AI workshop, or product brainstorm—ask not just, *"What will people use?"* Ask also, *"What will people recognize as their own?"*

Because the future isn't just built. In cultures like ours, it's also **remembered**.

Aarti of Innovation – A Poetic, Ceremonial Finale (Aka 'Final Thoughts')

Dear Reader,

Thank you—for walking this peer journey of Dharmic innovation. Across 108 principles, we have not merely studied strategies or frameworks—we've rekindled a relationship with our ancestral intelligence. Through the stories of Hanuman's leap, Vishwakarma's vision, Krishna's wisdom, and the village potter's ingenuity, we've remembered that innovation is not new—it is **Nitya**, eternal. It lives in our temples, kitchens, fields, and families. It's coded into our chants and passed through our touch.

What we explored is more than design thinking—it is **Dharma-thinking**. A way of seeing the world not as a problem to fix, but as a sacred system to serve, evolve, and harmonize with. Innovation then becomes a prayer. Prototyping becomes a form of *tapasya*. Product-market fit becomes a form of *seva*. And failure—just another *yuga* in the soul's unfolding design.

You've now seen that the wisdom of India—its myths, its mothers, its monks, its markets—is a wellspring of regenerative thought. The 108 takeaways were not just checklists; they were **mirrors** to your own intuitive genius. You may now recognize Vishnu not only in avatars but in agile pivots. You may see Ayurveda not only in healing but in human-centered design. You may sense that even a handful of cow dung carries more disruptive potential than a stack of venture decks—if seen through the lens of reverence and resourcefulness.

What's next?

Don't rush. Let this digest like a slow-cooked **kheer**, not a tweet thread. Reflect. Pause. Walk barefoot. Build what feels aligned. Break what blocks your spirit. Reclaim rituals. Reimagine systems. Collaborate not just to scale, but to soulfully serve.

Most of all, **trust yourself**. Your curiosity is sacred. Your heritage is valid. Your ancestors didn't just survive—they innovated beautifully, constantly, and compassionately. Now it is your turn.

Thank you for being part of this shared *yatra*—this pilgrimage of reawakening. May you innovate with clarity, build with care, and live your Dharma with joy.

With gratitude and respect,

The Dharma Innovation Collective